DAKINI ACTIVITY

The Dynamic Play of Awakening

RANGJUNG YESHE BOOKS ❖ WWW.RANGJUNG.COM

PADMASAMBHAVA ❖ *Treasures from Juniper Ridge* ❖ *Advice from the Lotus-Born* ❖
Dakini Teachings ❖ *Following in Your Footsteps: The Lotus-Born Guru in Nepal*
❖ *Following in Your Footsteps: The Lotus-Born Guru in India*

PADMASAMBHAVA AND JAMGÖN KONGTRÜL ❖ *The Light of Wisdom, Vol. 1, Vol. 2,
Vol. 3, Secret, Vol. 4, & Vol. 5*

PADMASAMBHAVA, CHOKGYUR LINGPA, JAMYANG KHYENTSE WANGPO, TULKU
URGYEN RINPOCHE, ORGYEN TOBGYAL RINPOCHE, AND OTHERS ❖
Dispeller of Obstacles ❖ *The Tara Compendium* ❖ *Powerful Transformation* ❖
Dakini Activity

YESHE TSOGYAL ❖ *The Lotus-Born*

DAKPO TASHI NAMGYAL ❖ *Clarifying the Natural State*

TSELE NATSOK RANGDRÖL ❖ *Mirror of Mindfulness* ❖ *Heart Lamp* ❖
Empowerment and Samaya

CHOKGYUR LINGPA ❖ *Ocean of Amrita* ❖ *The Great Gate* ❖ *Skillful Grace* ❖
Great Accomplishment ❖ *Guru's Heart Practices*

TRAKTUNG DUDJOM LINGPA ❖ *A Clear Mirror*

JAMGÖN MIPHAM RINPOCHE ❖ *Gateway to Knowledge, Vol. 1, Vol. 2, Vol. 3,
& Vol. 4*

TULKU URGYEN RINPOCHE ❖ *Blazing Splendor* ❖ *Rainbow Painting* ❖
As It Is, Vol. 1 & Vol. 2 ❖ *Vajra Speech* ❖ *Repeating the Words of the Buddha* ❖
Dzogchen Deity Practice ❖ *Vajra Heart Revisited*

ADEU RINPOCHE ❖ *Freedom in Bondage*

KHENCHEN THRANGU RINPOCHE ❖ *Crystal Clear* ❖ *Songs of True Accomplishment*

CHÖKYI NYIMA RINPOCHE ❖ *Bardo Guidebook* ❖ *Collected Works of
Chökgyi Nyima Rinpoche, Vol. I & Vol. 2*

TULKU THONDUP ❖ *Enlightened Living*

ORGYEN TOBGYAL RINPOCHE ❖ *Life & Teachings of Chokgyur Lingpa* ❖
Straight Talk ❖ *Sublime Lady of Immortality*

DZIGAR KONGTRÜL RINPOCHE ❖ *Uncommon Happiness*

TSOKNYI RINPOCHE ❖ *Fearless Simplicity* ❖ *Carefree Dignity*

MARCIA DECHEN WANGMO ❖ *Dzogchen Primer* ❖ *Dzogchen Essentials* ❖
Quintessential Dzogchen ❖ *Confessions of a Gypsy Yogini* ❖ *Precious Songs of
Awakening Compilation*

ERIK PEMA KUNSANG ❖ *Wellsprings of the Great Perfection* ❖ *A Tibetan Buddhist
Companion* ❖ *The Rangjung Yeshe Tibetan-English Dictionary of Buddhist
Culture & Perfect Clarity*

CHOKGYUR LINGPA, JAMGÖN KONGTRÜL, JAMYANG KHYENTSE WANGPO,
ADEU RINPOCHE, AND ORGYEN TOBGYAL RINPOCHE ❖ *The Tara Compendium
Feminine Principles Discovered*

DAKINI
ACTIVITY

The Dynamic Play of Awakening

Padmasambhava
Chokgyur Lingpa
Chokling Pema Gyurmey
Dzigar Kongtrul Rinpoche
Jamgön Kongtrül the First
Jamyang Khyentse Wangpo
Karmey Khenpo Rinchen Dargye
Orgyen Tobgyal Rinpoche
Lama Putsi Pema Tashi
Tulku Urgyen Rinpoche

Translated by
Erik Pema Kunsang, Marcia Schmidt, and Others

Rangjung Yeshe
PUBLICATIONS

Rangjung Yeshe Publications
526 Entrada Drive, Apt. 201
Novato, CA, 94949 USA

Address emails to:
Rangjung Yeshe Publications
C/O Above

www.rangjung.com
www.lotustreasure.com

First paperback edition published in 2018
Printed in the United States of America

Publication data: ISBN-13: 978-0-9977162-7-6 (pbk)

Title: *Dakini Activity: The Dynamic Play of Awakening*

Padmasambhava, Chokgyur Lingpa, Chokling Pema Gyurmey,
Dzigar Kongtrul Rinpoche, Jamgön Kongtrül the First, Jamyang Khyentse Wangpo,
Karmey Khenpo Rinchen Dargye, Orgyen Tobgyal Rinpoche,
Lama Putsi Pema Tashi & Tulku Urgyen Rinpoche

1. Vajrayana/Yidam—Tradition of Pith Instructions
2. Buddhism—Tibet

Photos courtesy of Neten Chokling Rinpoche and Graham Sunstein

Cover Art by Lowell Boyers: lowellboyers.com

CONTENTS

PREFACE

Marcia Binder Schmidt

In retrospect, it is always enlightening to discover how misleading preconceptions are. For instance, take this mundane example: I was always intrigued by gypsies and had a very Hollywood view of them, based on seeing films with female gypsy characters like Dolores del Rio and Rita Hayworth. In Barcelona, many years later, when I actually saw my first real-life gypsy, she was obviously nothing like my stereotype—quite the contrary, and my small-minded preconceptions shattered instantly.

Likewise, concerning dakinis, until I worked on this book, I had a vague image of starlet types, moving gracefully and swiftly through space, jingling bells, sporting jewels and silks, and being thoroughly captivating. Although this may be a superficial description of how some dakinis appear to us, if we can even see them, wisdoms dakinis do not necessarily look or act like this at all. They are powerful forces to be reckoned with and to be somewhat feared. As I discovered, they are penultimate judges, who determine whether we practitioners have the correct view, mediation, and conduct. If they discover we do not, they hurl untold negative consequences on us in this life, the bardo, and the next life. Dakinis are definitely nothing like sorority sisters or good old girls. They are objects of deep respect and veneration. While sorority sisters and good old girls deserve all due respect as well, I want to underline our need to be aware of the dakinis' profundity.

However, if we yogis and yoginis have the proper view, meditation, and conduct, we'll find no better protectors and guides than wisdom dakinis. They are conduits for carrying out our dharma activities and will support us unceasingly, in this life, the bardo, and the next life. Hence, wisdom dakinis, like dharma proctectors, can be forces of great good or harm, depending on our qualities as practitioners. As with my simple misconceptions about gypsies, my faulty ideas about dakinis were destroyed. I came to deeply revere the perspicacity of these sublime beings and to develop a healthy, conscientious fear of them.

Dakini Activity is the final book in this series on the Three Roots, and its emphasis is on dakini practices. As a reminder, please consider that the lama is the source of blessings, the yidam is the source of accomplishments, and the dakinis and protectors are the source of activities. Of course, these divisions are like three lines drawn in the sky. To successfully undertake the activities, we need the blessings and accomplishments; we cannot achieve anything without them. There is absolutely no way that our ordinary, discursive minds can command the wisdom dakinis, or even mundane ones. They will not be summoned to act for a limited purpose, nor will they respond to those lacking realization. Unless we have the support of wisdom, blessings, and accomplishments, our attempts to send out light rays and hooks will be erratic. These emanations will dissolve into the void and be of little value. Even on a mundane level, if we want important and powerful people to heed our wishes, we need to at least be on their level. A beggar cannot command a king.

That brings us back to the essential point: We need to rely on the powerful alchemical principles of deity, mantra, and samadhi. Ideally, we would allow the indivisible practices of development and completion stages to unfold from within the state of rigpa. However, since this is not possible for most of us, we at least need to imagine ourselves as the central figure in whichever mandala we are creating. Then, from within a state of samadhi, we would recite the mantras and enact the activities, ensuring that our purpose is consistently altruistic, not selfish or ordinary. We are enjoining these deities for dharmic purposes, to attract—and, in the case of Kurukulle practice, to magnetize—teachers, teachings, the ability to understand and engage the teachings, wealth, and all positive circumstances, for the benefit of the Dharma and sentient beings. If we have self-serving aims, we can beat the drum and ring the bells as much as we want, but the dakinis will not be summoned and will not carry out the activities. As with all practices, including these, even as juicy as they are, the motivation is to attain realization and proficiency for the benefit of beings and the Dharma. To paraphrase a famous quote: Endeavor to purify obscurations and gather the accumulations; to rely on any other means is delusion.

Thus, these dakini practices are being offered as sublime methods to play with dynamic energy. Sometimes they will be captivating, and at other times terrifying, but never mundane or ordinary! Our aim should be to first gain control over our own fickle minds. Then we will be empowered to turn our minds toward pacifying, increasing, magnetizing, and subjugating all outer and inner phenomena for the greater good. Here are some golden bricks on the path toward enlightenment. Tread lightly, steadfastly, and with great amazement. May the blessings and accomplishments accompany us practitioners, as we seek the guidance of the dakinis.

Kurukulle

INTRODUCTION

Orgyen Tobgyal Rinpoche

In the Indian languages, the word *dakini* connotes someone who is not quite human, not an ordinary girl or woman. The image it conveys is a little scary: a blood-drinker with fangs, red hair, long nails, and so forth, who can perform a few miracles now and then. In India, generally speaking, there are quite a few of them, especially in the twenty-four sacred places and valleys, and particularly in Dhumathala, which is the most eminent among all the sacred places. This is, shall we say, the capital of the dakinis. There is also a place in Pakistan, which seems to be the present-day region of Uddiyana, where a lot of women have facial hair resembling a mustache. They are naturally somewhat fierce and have certain tricks, or miracles, they can play, just by their nature. So the word generally refers to some kind of witch.

Dakini is translated into Tibetan as *khandro*, which doesn't have exactly the same meaning. The Tibetan connotation of khandro is "great gals," but in India if you call somebody a dakini, they will scratch your face and get angry, as it implies somebody who eats flesh, drinks blood, and casts spells. Most of the witches in Uddiyana could fly through the air. That's why they're called "sky-farers," or khandros, but I hear that these days only a few remain.

There are various types of dakinis, such as wisdom, karma, charnel-ground, and flesh-eating dakinis. The wisdom dakini, according to the Sarma schools, is Vajravarahi, or Dorje Phagmo in Tibetan. According to the Nyingma school, she is Samantabhadri, and so forth. The other primary wisdom dakinis, according to the Nyingma traditions, are the eight consorts of the eight great herukas and the five consorts of the five male buddhas. Among the five buddha families, the males represent the *upaya* aspect, skillful means, while the females represent the *prajñā* aspect, insight.

There's also a dakini that is not necessarily a wisdom dakini or a flesh-eating dakini: She is known as the Queen of Dharmadhatu, Ekajati. Also, there are five classes of karma dakinis, corresponding to the four activities of pacifying, increasing, magnetizing, and subjugating as well as the supreme activity. The charnel-ground dakinis are the eight sisters, and so forth.

Those are the main ones, the chiefs of the one hundred thousand different types. In short, every woman is a dakini. They're more intelligent than men and more sharp-minded. Nevertheless, they seem to think more; in other words, they have more plans, but more worries too.

Each of the main dakinis has a sadhana practice. *The Padma Khandro* practice belongs to the cycle of the Lotus Family of Speech, *Pema Sung,* which has many inconceivable sadhanas. Among these, some are for the *yab,* or male aspect, and others are for the *yum,* or female aspect. While many vast collections of extensive sadhanas exist, they can be condensed into the sadhanas of the Three Roots, the lama, yidam, and dakini. The lama is the source of blessings, the yidam is the source of accomplishment, and the dakini is the source of activities. The dakini carries out the activities for the lama and yidam. The ultimate view of the tantras, in both the new and old schools, is that the blessings from the male are received more quickly through the female. Once you obtain the blessings and achieve the accomplishment, you need to make use of them; enacting them is called the activity. In other words, the virtue of blessings and accomplishment is the activity, which is the dakini. Buddhists and Hindus alike say that the female deity is swifter than the male deity in bestowing blessings and accomplishments.

The ultimate yidam for the Kagyüs is Chakrasamvara in the male aspect and his consort Vajravarahi in the female aspect. Most Kagyü lamas have received the blessings based upon Vajravarahi and attained accomplishment through her. The Indian Pandita Naropa, the Tibetan Lotsawa Marpa, Jetsun Milarepa, Dakpo Dawa Shunnu, and others received the extraordinary blessings of inner heat, *tummo,* and attained the coemergent state of Mahamudra based on Vajravarahi.

Practitioners do the recitation-meditation for Chakrasamvara during the development and completion stage practices. At the time of the extraordinary practices, they do the outer, inner, and secret recitations of Vajravarahi. After finishing those, they train in the *Six Doctrines of Naropa:* tummo, illusory body, luminosity, dream yoga, bardo, and transference of consciousness, *powa.* Accomplishing the vital point of these and attaining the supreme accomplishment of Mahamudra are based on Vajravarahi.

According to this tradition, the ultimate wisdom is realized by relying on the example wisdom. If you want to practice the path of great bliss, based on the power of the channels, winds, and essences, then the skillful means of the female aspect is the vital point. In other words, the practice connected to the vase empowerment is the male aspect, while the more profound parts—the secret and wisdom-knowledge empowerments— are connected to the female aspect of sadhana, which is Vajravarahi in the Kagyü lineages. It is taught that, although Milarepa and his disciple Gampopa had various yidams, they attained accomplishment primarily through Vajravarahi practice connected with the second and third empowerments.

In the Sakya tradition, one of the principal yidams is the male Hevajra, whose female counterpart is Khechari (Kachoma), a form of Vajravarahi. The Sakyas practice the path and fruition tradition, *Lamdre,* transmitted by the great mahasiddha Virupa, through a golden chain of masters. However, in this lineage, as well, receiving the blessings and attaining extraordinary realization in this life or in the bardo, relies on consort practice, based on Khechari. A rain of *sindura*, flowers, and consorts will accompany awakening. All the realized masters of this tradition have practiced in this way. One of the great Sakya masters, Sachen, attained accomplishment through receiving the blessings of Khechari. For instance, at the time of death, he did not leave a corpse behind but went directly in his body to the celestial realms. This mode of departure is depicted as climbing a staircase that descends from above. I'm not exactly sure what that looks like and how it functions, but it definitely works. Having attained this siddhi, he received a lot of pith transmissions through Khechari. The Gelugpa also practice a form of Vajravarahi.

The Nyingmas have a red form of Vajravarahi and a black one, *Tromo Nagmo*. This black form is the exalted deity of many past vidyadharas, who practiced a sadhana revealed by Nyang Ral Nyima Ozer. The biography style supplication to Jamyang Khyentse Wangpo recounts that when he did the retreat of the black Vajravarahi, his skull cup started to blaze with fire, becoming so hot he couldn't touch it. A large number of sadhanas are now based on Troma Nagmo. *Yumka Dechen Gyalmo,* revealed by Jigme Lingpa, also has a form of Vajravarahi.

Kurukulle belongs to the family of Vajravarahi and Arya Tara. For Arya Tara, the dharmakaya is the great mother Prajñāparamita; the sambhokagaya is Arya Tara; and the nirmanakaya is the infinite manifestations, as stated in the Tara tantras. There are one hundred and eight main Tara sadhanas. Within these, the outer emanation is Kurukulle, Lhamo Rigzinma, and the inner emanation is Lhamo Uma. Within the Tara emanations, the inner aspect is the magnetizing female deity, Kurukulle, Lhamo Rigzinma.

Other dakini sadhanas belong to a cycle of six dakini practices known as *Zurza,* the personal practice of the princess of Zur. She was Prince Damdzin's consort when Padmasambhava was in Tibet. These six practices include the outer Tara, the inner Vajravarahi, the secret Sangwa Yeshe, the most secret Mandarava, and *thatness* Yeshe Tsogyal, as well as a guru sadhana.

Additionally, the *Rinchen Terdzod* contains the Padma Khandro practice of Rongzom Mahapandita, an emanation of Vairochana, which Jamyang Khyentse Wangpo rediscovered, and the *Seven Profound Teachings* on Kurukulle. These are the most well-known in the Nyingma tradition. One of Tertön Sogyal's terma also has a Padma Khandro sadhana that is practiced in Serta in eastern Tibet. In short, in Tibet, both the Kama and Terma traditions have Padma Khandro sadhanas with unbroken lineages and great blessings that are still practiced today.

Among the various treasure revealers, very few have dakini sadhanas. As I have heard it said, this is due to the dakini practices being very profound and the dakinis being kind of stingy with their teachings. They don't really want to let go of them that easily. Some auspicious coincidence has to fall into place perfectly before they're willing to pass on such teachings, and that doesn't happen so readily. Most tertöns have experienced a lot of trouble with trying to land a dakini terma, and they are rarely successful.

For instance, Chokgyur Lingpa was predicted to go to Karpo Drak, the White Cliff in Bhutan, where he was to reveal a very grand terma called the *Khandro Gongdü, the Embodiment of the Realization of All Dakinis.* If he had succeeded in doing this, it would have ensured that all his activity would have reached completion; however, somebody interfered, so he wasn't able to, and a big obstacle to his life arose as a result. In the prophecy, it also said that there's a connection between the *Khandro Gongdü* and his other Dzogchen terma called the *Dzogchen Desum, the Three Sections of Dzogchen.* It says that if he had established the *Dzogchen Desum* in writing, it would have become possible to also decode the *Khandro Gongdü*, and if both of them had been brought into this world at the same time, a huge number of people would have attained rainbow body.[1]

Chokgyur Lingpa's daughter, Mayum Könchok Paldrön, had a parchment from her father with one of the dakini scripts that had never been decoded. After she died, her son Tersey Tulku inherited it. When Tersey Tulku met with Dilgo Khyentse Rinpoche,[2] he asked Rinpoche to decode it. This turned out to be the sadhana for the eight dakini consorts of the eight herukas. It was eventually written down, but then the lineage was broken. Some years ago, when I went back to eastern Tibet, I got hold of the text, but the empowerment lineage no longer exists.

What is the purpose and benefit of dakini practice? It has outer, inner, secret, and innermost ways to magnetize. The outer way is to magnetize those with and without form, humans, and nonhumans. For humans, the three categories of male, female, and neuter all need to be brought under control. The males subdivide into five families, or as in the Indian system, castes of kings, brahmins, businessmen, workers, and untouchables. The females also group into five families: padma, conch, elephant, drawing, and deer. Many beings live in the three planes of existence—the gods above, the nagas below the ground, and the nonhumans in between— and these make up the eight categories of haughty spirits. We magnetize them all. In addition, we magnetize the five primary elements.

Based on controlling the outer elements, we inwardly magnetize the inner elements, the five aggregates, and *ayatanas*. When we gain control over the five elements outwardly and the five aggregates, ayatanas, and inner elements inwardly, then we subdue the five poisons, which transform into the five wisdoms. This is the inner way to magnetize.

Secretly, when we gain mastery over the moving winds, the arranged channels, and the blissful bindus, the wisdom of the three vajras arises. Innermost magnetizing means gaining mastery over mind. Mind is what we are trying to control, and right now we do not have this mastery. As for the fruition of magnetizing, I will not tell that now. However, the reason we practice a magnetizing deity is to attain this power of magnetizing.

It is essential to know that you need to dissolve duality in order to accomplish any deity. To attain this within the structure of a sadhana practice, you progress through the stages of approach, close approach, accomplishment, and great accomplishment. That is in the extensive way, which you can condense into approach, accomplishment, and activities. The aspect of approach means the deity is very close. Accomplishment occurs when you recognize that you and the deity are inseparable, which we call realizing one taste. Once you accomplish the deity, you can enact the infinite activities related to pacifying, increasing, magnetizing, and subjugating.

In the Kurukulle sadhana in particular, the vital point is to fulfill the activities. The work, or activity, of the deity is the display of enlightened body, speech, and mind. Individuals who cannot benefit from peaceful and increasing activity can be helped by magnetizing and subjugating activity, which is unique to the unexcelled secret Vajrayana. The other vehicles do not have magnetizing and subjugating activity. Many methods are available for enacting peaceful and increasing activities. However, for completely unruly beings, or ones with strong desire, anger, impure perception, or no faith, only the Secret Mantra activities of magnetizing and subjugating can tame them.

Kurukulle enacts the magnetizing activity that brings profound benefit rapidly. Practicing this sadhana is what we need to accomplish, and to do this we need the empowerment. As it is said, "Without the empowerment, we cannot attain the accomplishments." In short, dakini practice expedites the process of attaining supreme and common siddhis. It is also especially effective for clearing damages in samayas. As I mentioned before, once you receive the blessings through the guru sadhana and attain accomplishments through the yidam practice, you make use of those by engaging the activity through the dakini practice.

Padma Khandro Mandala

KURUKULLE PRACTICE

Padmasambhava and Chokgyur Lingpa

KURUKULLE PRELIMINARIES

The Easily Applied Sadhana and Preliminaries for Padma Dakini

According to the Profundity of Longevity within the Seven Profound Teachings

Composed and Arranged by Jamgön Kongtrül

Namo guru dheva dhakiniye

Within the Profundity of Longevity *practice of the Three Roots,*
These are the preliminaries for the magnetizing Padma Dakini.
In accordance with the general framework of the Seven Profound Teachings,
They were extracted for easy application.
If you wish to practice them, then say,

1. LINEAGE SUPPLICATION[3]

Dechen pemey rigchok nangtha ye
Jigten wangchuk pema gargyi wang
Khamsum wangdzey tachok yabyum la
Solwa debso nangsem wangyur shog

Supreme head of the lotus family of great bliss, Amitabha,
Lord of the lotus display, Lokeshvara,
Magnetizer of the three realms, Hayagriva and consort,
I supplicate you; may appearance and mind be magnetized.

Nangsi zilnon pema gyalpoi shab
Yingchuk yeshe khandro tsogyalma
Ngadag chogyal tridey yabsey la
Solwa debso nangsem wangyur shog

Splendorous subjugator of all that appears and exists, Pema
  Gyalpo,
Dhatvishvari wisdom dakini, Tsogyalma,
Lord and Dharma King Trisong Deütsen and son,
I supplicate you; may appearance and mind be magnetized.

Drö dul trül pey ter chen chokgyur ling
Kabab lungthob tsagyu lama dang
Yidam khandro damchen tersung la
Solwa debso nangsem wangyur shog

Incarnated great treasure revealer, tamer of beings, Chokgyur
  Lingpa,
Root and lineage masters, receivers of the transmission and
  prophesy,
Yidams, dakinis, protectors, and guardians of the terma,
I supplicate you; may appearance and mind be magnetized.

Rangrig gyurmey yedrol lhunjam ngang
Rigtsal nangsi khordey wangdu due
Nangsem nyimey nyagchig chokui long
Jajey tsoldrub drelwey dingthob shog

In the spontaneous and all-pervasive state of primordially free and
  unchanging self-awareness,
May the expression of awareness, what appears and exists, samsara
  and nirvana, be magnetized.
Within the single expanse of dharmakaya, the nonduality of
  appearance and mind,
May I attain the confidence free from subject and object, effort and
  cultivation.[4]

(From Ngakso:[5])

Om hayagriva hung phet
Rangnyi kechig gi pema heruka pema dang thoetrak dzinpey kur
gyur

---

5 *Ocean of Amrita*

DAKINI ACTIVITY

Dei thugka ney ram yam kham troepey madagpey
    ngoedzin tamchey sektor jang
Tongpey ngangley sangchui tengdu
Ma surya mandal
Nyima la neypey hung yig marpo
Sapha rana phet sangha rana hung
Troe due yongsu gyurpa ley
Om pema maha krodhi shvari hung phet
Tromo wangchukma marmo drilbu dang bhanmar
    dzinpey kur gyur

Oм HAYAGRIVA HUNG PHAT

In a single instant, I become the form of Padma Heruka, holding a lotus flower and a skull cup filled with blood.

RAM YAM KHAM

Emanating from my heart center, these seed syllables burn, scatter, and purify all fixation on things as being real. From the state of emptiness, upon the sanctifying water,

MA SURYA MANDAL

Arises the red letter HUNG situated upon a sun disc.

SAPHA RANA PHAT SANGHA RANA HUNG

From the transformation of emanating and absorbing,

Oм PADMA MAHA KRODHI SHVARI HUNG PHAT

It assumes the form of red Krodhishvari, holding a bell and a fresh skull cup.

Imagining this, touch with the one-pointed mudra and consecrate one hundred and eight times, saying,

Oм MAHA KRODHI SHVARI SARVA DRABAYAM SHODHAYA OM AH HUNG HRIH THA

Then say,

Tromo wangchukmai rangzhin gyi chui dul trarab tu gyur

It turns into subtle particles of water, the nature of Krodhishvari.

Imagining this, say,

OM MAHA KRODHI SHVARI SARVA DRABAYAM SHODHAYA HUNG
PHAT

*In this way, you sanctify by sprinkling everything: yourself, the place, and
the articles. At the beginning of any practice, you should perform these acts of
sanctifying and sprinkling. (End of insert from Ngakso.)*

KARTOR — WHITE TORMA
FOR THE LOCAL DEITY

Burn, scatter, and wash away the torma, saying,

RAM YAM KHAM

**Tongpey ngang ley drung ley rinpochey noe yangshing gyachewa
nangdu torma khadog driro nupa phunsum tsogpar gyur**

From within emptiness, BHRUM becomes an open and vast jewel
vessel, within which is a torma with perfect color, smell, taste, and
potency.

To consecrate it, say three times,

OM AH HUNG

To invite, say,

BHUMIPATI SAPARIVARA BENZA SAMA DZAH

To dedicate it, say,

BHUMIPATI SAPARIVARA OM AKARO MUKHANG SARVA DHARMA
NA ADINUPEU NATOTA OM AH HUNG PHAT SOHA

Gangdag dirney lha dang lu
Nojin sinpo am shendag la
Kyilkhor dondu sachok di
Dagshu kyekyi tsaldu sol

Whoever dwells at this site, devas or nagas,
Yakshas, rakshas, or anyone else,
I request this place from you for the mandala.
So please give it over to me.

Request in this way three times and imagine that permission is given.

2. THE TERMA ROOT TEXT FOR REFUGE AND BODHICHITTA

Namo:

Gyalkun duezuk lama khandro mar:
Gupey kyabchi semchen kundon du:
Sangye tenpa rinchen kyongwa la:
Dina sheyching drubpa jepa yi:

Gendun dupey denam duwa dang:
Chokyi chakyen malu drubpey chi:
Lama khandro drubpar damcha wey:
Kawa meypar dudir drubpar shog:

In the guru dakini, who embodies all the victorious ones,:
I respectfully take refuge. And for the sake of all sentient beings,:
I pledge to accomplish the guru dakini,:
In order to sustain the precious Dharma teachings:
And gather the sublime Sangha,:
Who explain and practice the Dharma:
And produce all the necessities for Dharma practice.:
So, without any difficulty, may I achieve this right now.:

Chant that three times.

DZAH HUNG BAM HOH

Tsogshing nam rangla thimpar gyur

The entire field of accumulation dissolves into me.

Consecrate the torma for the obstructing spirits and dedicate it with the mantra.[6]

3. COMMANDING THE OBSTRUCTING SPIRITS

(From Ngakso:*)*

OM SOBHAVA SHUDDHO SARVA DHARMA SOBHAVA SHUDDHO HANG

Tongpey ngang ley dhrung ley rinpochei noe yangshing gyachewey nangdu torma khadog driro nuepa phunsum tsogpar gyur

From the state of emptiness, BHRUM becomes an immense and gigantic jewel vessel. The torma within it has perfect color, fragrance, taste, and potency.

While performing the garuda mudra, say three times,

OM AH HUNG

And then consecrate, saying,

HA HOH HRIH

Summon the guests with the hook mudra, saying,

OM SARVA BHUTA AHKAR KAYA DZAH

Then dedicate the torma by saying three times,

OM SARVA BIGHANEN NAMAH SARVA TATHAGATE BHAYO BISHO MUKHEBHE SARVA THAKHAM UTGATE SAPARANA IMAM GAGANA KHAM GRIHANA DAM BALINGTE SOHA

(End of insert from Ngakso.)

Hrih hung
Ngani rangjung pema heruka
Khordey kunla wangyur dorjei ka
Mada togtrul barchey gegkyi tsok
Yetong tsadrel nyugmey yingsu deng
Sarva bighanen gaccha phet

Hrih hung
Hosts of obstacle-makers and obstructors, concepts and confusion,
Do not transgress my vajra command, as the self-arisen Padma
    Heruka,
Who has mastered all of samsara and nirvana.
Disperse into innate space, primordially empty and rootless.
Sarva bighanen gaccha phat

4. Drawing the Boundary for Protection

Hung
Doney namdag yeshe kyilkhor dir
Tsendzin trulpey barchey ming yang mey
Nangdrag togtsok lha ngag Ösel ying
Jazer chagtsen meyphung barwey tam
Benza raksha raksha hung

Hung
Within this primordial mandala of pure wisdom,
Not even the words for clinging to concepts and deluded obstacles
    exist.
Sights, sounds, and thoughts are deity, mantra, and the space of
    luminosity.
It is filled with rainbow rays, attributes, and a blazing mass of fire.
Vajra raksha raksha hung

5. The Gesture of Homage, Confession of Faults, and Taking the Oath

Hoh
Thabshey go ye rangrig lhashel jal
Lodey nyimey tokpey donchak tsal
Trulpey wang gi thadey dzinpa shag
Midrel drubpey dorjei yardam zung
Benza samaya hung

Hoh
Opening the door of means and knowledge and meeting the deity
    of self-awareness,
I pay the ultimate homage of realizing nonduality beyond concepts.
I confess my confused fixation on separateness
And vow to keep the vajra oath of constant practice.
Vajra samaya hung

6. Bringing Down the Great Resplendence of Wisdom

Hrih
Dechen barwa wang gi phodrang ney
Gyusum lama zhi tro yidam lha
Neysum khandro chokyong damtsig chen
Kyepar pema daki tsokhor chey

Hrih
From the shining palace of magnetizing great bliss,
Gurus of the three lineages, peaceful and wrathful yidam deities,
Dakinis of the three abodes, dharma protectors possessing the
    samaya,
And especially Padma Dakini, chief figure, and entourage,

Dungshug drakpoi thugdam gyukul na
Drubney kyilkhor dila jinchen phob
Drubchog naljor dagla wangchen kur
Drubdzey yeshe chag gyar jingyi lop

With great yearning, I call upon you, invoking your promise.
Please bestow a great resplendence upon this site of sadhana.
Confer the great empowerment upon me, a yogi of the supreme
   sadhana.
Consecrate the articles of sadhana as wisdom forms.

Nangdrag chokun rigpey wangdu due
Khordey nyamnyi thigle chenpor dzog
Doney gyurmey dechen Ösel ngang
Lhundzog dalwa chenpoi jinphob chig
Benza gyana abeshaya a ah

May sights and sounds, all phenomena, come under the sway of
   awareness.
May samsara and nirvana be perfected as the great sphere of
   equality.
Within this primordially unchanging state of luminous great bliss,
May you bestow the resplendence of the great, all-encompassing
   spontaneous perfection.

VAJRA JNANA ABESHAYA A AH

7. TERMA ROOT TEXT FOR CONSECRATING THE OFFERINGS

OM VAJRA AMRITA KUNDALI HUNG PHAT

Cleanse, saying,

RAM YAM KHAM

Purify, saying,

OM SOBHAVA (and so forth)[7]

Tongpey ngang ley pema barwey noe
Om ah hung ley chopey jedrag ni
Sosor selshing yeshe chotrin ni
Dewa kyeching yitrok gugpa yi
Nampar charshing nupa chendu gyur

Om ah hung⸰
Benza sapharana kham⸰

Within the state of emptiness appears a shining lotus vessel.⸰
From om ah hung, the different types of offerings⸰
Are individually manifest as a cloud of wisdom offerings,⸰
Appearing in potent forms⸰
That generate bliss, fascinate, and magnetize.⸰
OM AH HUNG⸰
VAJRA SAPHARANA KHAM⸰

By uttering this mantra three times,
Consecrate the offerings and enter the actual sadhana.

In accord with the wish of the supreme Choying,
The Nirmanakaya of Palnge,
This was written by Chimey Tennyi Lingpa[8]
Directly as it came to mind.
By the virtue of this may personal experience be brought under control.
May virtuous goodness increase.

THE SADHANA OF THE LOTUS DAKINI FOR MAGNETIZING ACTIVITY

According to the Profundity of Longevity within the Seven Profound Teachings

The Terma Root Text Revealed by Chokgyur Lingpa

ཨོཾ༔

I, Padma, who devotedly bows down to the mother of the victorious ones,༔
Will teach the sadhana of the Lotus Dakini for magnetizing activity,༔
In order to benefit future upholders of the teachings.༔
First, go to a secluded place,༔
Which should have red soil and cliffs or rocks with sharp edges.༔
Draw a crescent-shaped mandala with a perfect door in the center,༔
With an enclosure of lotus flowers, vajras, and flames of fire.༔

In the middle, draw an eight-petaled flower, and in its center,༔
Draw a red lotus flower marked with hooks.༔

Upon a manjikha, *within a copper vase*༔
Fill wine and the three magnetizing substances,༔
The twenty-one general substances, and the five nectars.༔
Adorn it with a choker of red cloth, and sew a top ornament,༔
Peacock feathers, and red flowers.༔

The torma of dough made from various grains mixed with wine༔
Should be adorned with butter-flowers and red hooks༔
Formed by the hands of a beautiful girl.༔
Sprinkle fragrant ointment on this cubit-sized torma.༔
With eight similar types, beautify with a canopy of red silk.༔

Moreover, mentally create and arrange similar articles༔
As well as the outer, inner, and secret offerings.༔
You, yourself, should wear red ornaments, garlands, and clothing.༔

Imagine then that all the victorious ones are perfectly present in the sky before you (and say),[89]

Namo

Gyalkun duezuk lama khandro mar

Gupey kyabchi semchen kundon du

Sangye tenpa rinchen kyongwa la

Dina sheyching drubpa jepa yi

Gendun dupey denam duwa dang

Chokyi chakyen malu drubpey chi

Lama khandro drubpar damcha wey

Kawa meypar dudir drubpar shog

Namo In the guru dakini, who embodies all the victorious ones,
I respectfully take refuge. And for the sake of all sentient beings,
I pledge to accomplish the guru dakini,
In order to sustain the precious Dharma teachings
And gather the sublime Sangha,
Who explain and practice the Dharma
And produce all the necessities for Dharma practice.
So, without any difficulty, may I achieve this right now.

Chant this three times and generate the mind set upon enlightenment.
Give a torma to the obstructors and issue them the command.
Having performed the general framework of the preliminaries, such as the protection circle, (then say,)

Hrih

Chonam mimik kadag ngang

Magag nyingjei rolpa ley

Hrih yig marpo obar gyur

Deley otro noechu jang

HRIH

In the primordially pure state, devoid of conceptualizing
   phenomena,
The play of compassion is unobstructed.
From it appears the brilliant red letter HRIH,
Sending out light that purifies the world and beings.

E yam ra sum keng ram nam༔
Tropey jungwa rimtsek teng༔
Dhrung ley rinchen zhelyey khang༔
Gyendang koepa yongdzog nang༔

E ʏᴀᴍ ʀᴀ ꜱᴜᴍ ᴋᴇɴɢ ʀᴀᴍ ɴᴀᴍ༔
Are emanated as the gradual layers of elements.༔
Upon them, bhrum becomes a celestial palace of jewels,༔
With perfect adornments and decorations.༔

Pema dabgye gesar dang༔
Dabmar pema marpo dang༔
Nyimey denla hrih mar gu༔
Yong gyur pemay chagkyur gyur༔

Inside is a lotus flower with eight petals and anthers.༔
On each petal is a red lotus.༔
On the thrones of sun discs are nine red hrih༔
That transform into lotus hooks.༔

Tewar hrih tsen omar bar༔
Donnyi jeydu ozhu ley༔
Pema khandro tsokhor gu༔
Tamchey pema marpo dok༔

Their centers, marked with ʜʀɪʜ, shine with red light.༔
Fulfilling the two aims,༔
The light gathers back and the hooks melt into light,༔
Becoming the nine lotus dakinis—the chief figure and entourage.༔
All of them are the color of the red lotus flower.༔

Zhelchig chagzhi chagkyu dang༔
Zhagpa pemey dazhu dzin༔
Dzeshing chakpey nyamchen la༔
Dardang rinchen rupey gyen༔
Zhabnyi garthab rolpa yi༔
Omar barwey una zhug༔

They have one face and four arms, holding a hook,༔
A noose, and a lotus bow and arrow.༔
With expressions that are attractive and passionate,༔

They are adorned with silks and jewel-and-bone ornaments.
Their two legs perform dance movements,
While they stand amidst a radiant red effulgence.

Gozhir gosung phomo gye
Zhelchig chagnyi chagkyu dang
Zhagpa dzinching garthab gyur

At the four gates are the eight male and female gatekeepers,
With one face and two arms, holding a hook and noose
And performing dance movements.

Chirol pema dorjei gur
Ozer mephung barwar sel
Kusung thuksu jinlab te
Yeshe ngayi wangdzog shog
Om ah hung
Om hung tram hrih ah

Outside is a dome of lotus flowers and vajras,
Manifest with beams of light and a blazing mass of fire.
Consecrated as body, speech, and mind,
May I perfect the empowerment of the five wisdoms.
OM AH HUNG
OM HUNG TRAM HRIH AH

Thukmey nyiteng hrih yig ley o troepey rangzhin gyi neyney
    gompa dang drawey yeshepa samgyi mikhyabpa chendrang

Upon a sun disc in the lower part of the heart, the letter HRIH
sends out light inviting an inconceivable number of wisdom beings, who resemble the visualized ones, to come from the innate
abode.

Hrih
Choying kyewa meypa ley
Magag longcho dzogkur zheng
Thugje natsok nangdzey ma
Khandroi tsognam sheksu sol
Khandroi tsognam shekney kyang

Leykyi drebu chipar dzoe
Pema dakini saparivara benza sama dzah
Dzah hung bam hoh
Samaya tishtha lhen

Hrih
Out of the nonarising dharmadhatu,
Appear in your unobstructed sambhogakaya forms.
Ladies who manifest in manifold compassionate ways,
Hosts of dakinis, please come!
Hosts of dakinis, having arrived,
Show the result of your activity!
Padma dakini saparivara vajra sama jah
Jah hung bam hoh
Samaya tishtha lhan

Hrih
Dirsham pema barwa ru
Damye nyimey shugsu sol
Yeshe yingley gakpa mey
Chiryang trul la chaktsal lo
Atipu ho pratibhu ho

Hrih
Upon the shining lotus flowers arranged here,
Please be seated as nondual samaya and wisdom beings.
I pay homage to you, who manifest in all ways,
Unobstructedly, from the space of wisdom.
Atipu hoh pratibhu hoh

Hung
Rabjam shingkun gangwey chotrin ni
Metog dupoe marmey drichab dang
Zhelsey rolmo zukdra driro rek
Tashi dzeytak gyalsi nampa dun
Gyalwey yumgyur khordang cheyla bul
Zheney dopey ngodrub tsaldu sol
Pema dakini saparivara pushpe dhupe aloke gendhe niwente
    shapta kamaguna mangalam ratna pudza hoh

HUNG

An offering cloud filling all the infinite realms

With flowers, incense, lamps, and perfume,

Edibles, music, forms, sounds, scents, tastes, and touchables,

The eight auspicious substances and symbols, and the seven royal
  possessions

I offer to you, mother of the buddhas, and your retinue.

Accept it and bestow the desired siddhis!

PADMA DAKINI SAPARIVARA PUSHPE DHUPE ALOKE GANDHE
NAIVIDYA SHAPTA KAMAGUNA MANGALAM RATNA PUDZA HOH

Nyimey jangchub semkyi dutsi dang
Chagmey rakta chagpey ney chenpo
Doeyon torma yeshe gyatsoi trin
Bullo gyepar zhela trinley dzoe
Maha amrita rakta balingta kharam khahi

The nectar of the nondual mind of enlightenment,

The rakta of nonattachment, the great site of passion,

The torma of sense pleasures, as an ocean-like cloud of wisdom,

I offer to you. Accept it joyfully and carry out your activity!

MAHA AMRITA RAKTA BALINGTA KHARAM KHAHI

Hrih
Dewey rangshin sempey tsog
Trultey gyepar trilpa yi
Dewey namgyur duma yi
Sangchoe dewey neyla rol
Aho mahasukha

OM AH HUNG

A LA LA HOH

A HANG[10]

HRIH

Emanating a host of sattvas, the nature of bliss,

And entwining with them joyfully,

Enjoy the secret offering, the site of bliss,

The manifold expressions of delight!

AHO MAHASUKHA

OM AH HUNG

A LA LA HOH

A HANG

Hrih

Dondam miyo dewa chenpoi ku

Chiryang nangwa dechen yungdrung lha

Dopey donkun nyurdu tsoldzey ma

Dorje tsunmoi tsogla chagtsal lo

HRIH

In the ultimate, unshakable form of great bliss,

Deity of unchanging great bliss, manifest in all ways,

As ladies who swiftly bestow all desired aims.

Gathering of vajra queens, to you I pay homage.

Meditate in that way, enjoining them to activity.

THE SAMADHI OF EMANATING AND ABSORBING

Lhamo namkyi thugkar nyima la neypey hrih yig
ley oezer marpo chagkyui yibchen troepey, gang
wangdu duewar doepey nying gar pogpa tsamgyi
do khablen gyi chagchey duepa tar wangdu
dueney lhamoi thugkai hrih la thimpar gyur

Imagine as follows:

The HRIH syllables situated on the sun discs in the heart centers
of the goddesses radiate red rays of light in the form of hooks.
By merely touching the heart centers of whomever they wish to
magnetize, those beings are brought under their power—just as
a magnet gathers together all iron filings—and dissolve into the
HRIH in the heart centers of the goddesses.

OM KURU KULLE HRIH SOHA

By reciting one hundred thousand, a suitable sign will occur. In your breaks, offer a torma, and enjoin the activities. At the end, the world and beings dissolve into the base,[11] *and the base itself dissolves into the heart center of the chief figure. Imagining that she dissolves into your own heart center, chant,*

OM PEMA DAKINI SIDDHI HUNG[12]

Recite this one thousand times, drink water from the vase, and dedicate the virtue.

SAMAYA. SEAL. SEAL. SEAL.

I, Orgyen Chokgyur Dechen Lingpa, took this out of Yelphug Namkha Dzo in the company of the destined Sukha.

THE ESSENCE OF MAGNETIZING[13]

An Additional Manual for the Lotus Dakini within the Seven Profound Teachings

Extremely Profound — Seal of Secrecy

Padmasambhava and Chokgyur Lingpa

Hrih:
Dechen yeshe gyepey rangsuk ley:
Naljor lhamo yitrok wangdzey ma:
Gyalkun yeshe chigdue leytrung pey:
Zhelchig chakshi ma la chaktsal toe:

Hrih:
From the natural form of expanding the wisdom of great bliss,:
You appear as the enchanting and magnetizing yogini goddess.:
Born out of the combined wisdom of all the victorious ones,:
Lady with one face and four arms, I salute and offer praise to you.:

Gyalkun gyeyum dechen rigjey ma:
Nangsi wangdue mardzum chagpey nyam:
Pemey chagkyu zhagpa dazhu yi:
Khamsum wangdue dzey la chaktsal toe:

Kurukulle, consort who delights all the victorious ones,:
Your flushed, smiling expression of passion magnetizes all that
    appears and exists,:
With the lotus hook, noose, bow, and arrow.:
Magnetizer of the three realms, I salute and offer praise to you.:

---

13 Translated by Erik Pema Kunsang

Dechen lhamo gyepey yab gyur pa
Heruka pal khatvang ga la khyu
Chagpey obar trikpey u na gar
Sherab nyimey teng rol khyoe la due

As a khatvanga, you embrace the glorious heruka,
The lord who delights the goddess of great bliss.
Dancer within a mass of blazing, passionate radiance,
Who revels upon the sun disc of discriminating knowledge, I bow
    down to you.

Natsok moepey gyutrul rolpa ley
Rangdang drawey naljor gyekyi kor
Choktsam kuntu trulpa drangmey gye
Dorje tsunmoi tsok la chaktsal toe

Out of the magical display that suits various dispositions,
You are encircled by eight yoginis similar to you.
Sending out countless emanations in all directions,
Assembly of vajra queens, I salute and offer praise to you.

Hrih hrih
Sizhi yiguk naljor mayi tsok
Drubpo dag gi rangdon jangchub dang
Zhendon jawa leykyi khorlor tson
Dela naljor makun drokdzoe chik

Hrih hrih
Gathering of yoginis, captivators of samsaric existence and nirvanic
    peace,
I, the practitioner, exert myself in attaining enlightenment for the
    benefit of myself
And in constant activity for the welfare of others.
Yoginis, give your assistance!

Moegue wang gi lama wangdu due
Thoesam nyurwey damchoe wangdu due
Bag yoe wang gi gosum wangdu due
Nyingje wang gi drokun wangdu due

Through respect and devotion, magnetize a master.

Through swift learning and reflection, magnetize the sacred
    Dharma.

Through carefulness, magnetize the three gates.

Through compassion, magnetize all sentient beings.

Chagya wang gi rangsem wang du due
Dechen wang gi yeshe wang du due
Yeshe wang gi gyalkun wang du due
Jinlab wang gi chokyong wang du due

Through a mudra, magnetize my own mind.

Through great bliss, magnetize primordial wakefulness.

Through primordial wakefulness, magnetize all the victorious
    ones.

Through blessings, magnetize the dharma protectors.

Rigtsal wang gi nangsi wang du due
Ziji wang gi gyalpo wang du due
Damtsig wang gi khandro wang du due
Drakpey wang gi gyalkham wang du due

Through the expression of awareness, magnetize all that appears
    and exists.

Through majestic splendor, magnetize kingly rulers.

Through samaya, magnetize the dakinis.

Through renown, magnetize all countries.

Tenpey dondu thegchen gendun dang
Drophen chirdu lhalu misum dang
Longchoe chirdu seygoe nornam dang
Ngathang chirdu khorlob desi dang
Yithun drogdang nyandrak jorden sok
Sizhi palkun gyurwa wangdu due
Om kuru kulle hrih a nri tri ra sa saparshe basu washam kuru
    hung

For the benefit of the teachings, magnetize the Mahayana sangha.

For the benefit of beings, magnetize gods, nagas, and humans.

For the benefit of affluence, magnetize food, clothing, and wealth.

For the benefit of dominion, magnetize attendants, disciples, and
followers.ᔰ
Magnetize harmonious companions, fame, and abundance.ᔰ
In short, magnetize all the splendor of samsaric existence and
nirvanic peace.ᔰ

*This additional hidden praise and invocation of the Lotus Dakini was
translated from the secret dakini script by Chokgyur Lingpa. In the victorious
year of the chariot, it was combined from the handwriting of the great tertön
by a khenpo disciple[14] of the tertön himself. May it be virtuous.*

CONFESSION OF FAULTS

Hoh
Choekun doeney kyegag neydrel yang
Zhenchag trulpey nongpa chigyi pa
Sortog yeshe longdu zoezhey la
Sizhi wang gyur chenpor ug yung tsol

Hoh
Although all phenomena are originally beyond arising, dwelling,
    and ceasing,
Whatever I may have wronged out of clinging, attachment, and
    confusion,
Please forgive in the expanse of discriminating wisdom,
And assure me of the great mastery over existence and peace.

Repeat the Hundred Syllable mantra.

*Request the wisdom being visualized in front to remain in the shrine
image.*[15]

Dissolve the samaya being into you, by saying OM AH HUNG.
Let the self-visualization enter the luminosity by saying HUNG.
Re-emerge in the form of the deity by saying phat.

ASPIRATION

Dagzhen duesum sagpey gewa yi
Lungsem nangwa wangdu dueney kyang
Khordey kungyi khyabdag dewa che
Wangchen yabyum gophang nyurthob shog

By the virtue accumulated by me and others throughout the three
    times,
May the appearances of prana and mind be brought under control,

And may we quickly attain the state of the Great Mighty One and
consort,
The great, blissful nature encompassing all of samsara and nirvana.

UTTERANCE OF AUSPICIOUSNESS

Ema hoh
Rangnang pemo gyepey zhelmey khang
Rigtsal pema nampar rolpey lha
Sizhi wangdu dzeypey tashi dey
Doegu wangjey gelek palbar shog

EMA HOH
Deities of lotus display, the expression of awareness,
In the celestial palace of the blooming lotus, personal experience,
May your auspiciousness of mastering existence and peace
Blaze forth with the splendor and virtuous goodness of
magnetizing all desirable things.

Rangjung dagam wang gi phodrang du
Dewey dangjin pema rigkyi cham
Zagmey gawa kyilwey tashi dey
Doegu wangjey gelek palbar shog

Within the self-existing palace of the magnetizing crescent,
Consort of the lotus family, who yields forth the blissful luster,
May your auspiciousness of bringing in the unconditioned joy
Blaze forth with the splendor and virtuous goodness of
magnetizing all desirable things.

Chokley namgyal choezang dunsa ru
Jigten wangchuk lhachen tsogkyi je
Gangsam nyurdu gugpey tashi dey
Doegu wangjey gelek palbar shog

In the gathering hall of the eminent Dharma, victorious over all
opponents,
Lord of the world, Mahadeva, chief of the assembly,

May your auspiciousness of swiftly summoning whatever is wished
for
Blaze forth with the splendor and virtuous goodness of
magnetizing all desirable things.

Chirol yulnang thadag wangdu due
Lungsem trultog nang gi umar zhug
Gyurmey dechen dorje gargyi wang
Choying kunkyab chenpoi tashi shog

May all outer perceived objects be brought under control,
May the confused thinking of the prana-mind enter the inner
central channel,
And may the auspiciousness of the great, all-encompassing
dharmadhatu,
The unchanging great bliss of the Vajra Lord of Display, be
present.[16]

While chanting this, do not let your mind fall under the power of appearances; rather, sustain the experience and let it become the virtuous goodness of expanding the splendor of your heart.

This arose in my experience, although I have not untied the dakinis' seal of entrustment. For whatever I may have mistaken, I beg the gurus and dakinis for their forgiveness. Through this virtue, may we attain the form of the Lord of Display.

When separately practicing the Lotus Dakini of the New Treasures, Tersar Pema Khandro, *I saw the need for and felt the wish to compose an easily applied accessory text. Thus I, Padma Gargyi Wangchuk Tsal, spontaneously wrote this at Tsadra Rinchen Drak. May virtuous goodness increase.*

This is especially entrusted to the guardian of the teachings and his consort, so that unworthy people may not even see the text. Samaya. Seal of concealment.

INVOKING THE ACTIVITY OF LORD MAHADEVA AND CONSORT[17]

Arranged by Pema Gyurmey

In accordance with the oral teachings, prepare a torma, clean fruit, grains, silks, gold, silver, and so forth. Then cleanse, purify, and consecrate by saying,

RAM YAM KHAM
OM AH HUNG

Then imagine as follows:

Rang gi thugkai hrih ley oezer marpo troe
Lhachen wangchuk yabyum gyi thugkar phogpey ngongyi damcha
Jeysu drenney tsezhing dungwey tsuldu zhugpey jag pemey bugue
Tormey chue drangtey solwar gyur

The red beams of light radiating from the HRIH in my heart center strike the hearts of Lord Mahadeva and consort. Thus, they remember their former vow and remain with loving affection. Enjoying this torma, they consume its essence with the light of the hollow lotus of their tongues.

At the end of the mantra,[18] say,

SAPARIVARA IDAM BALINGTA KHAKHA KHAHI KHAHI
SARVA SIDDHI WASHAM KURU HOH

Accompanied by drum music and melodious tune, sing,

Hung
Dechen wang gi kyilkhor ney

---

17 Translated by Erik Pema Kunsang
18 OM MAHADEVA DZA
   UMA DEVI HRING HARINISA SIDDHI DZA

43

Khamsum kungyi yigug pa
Lhachen wangchuk umar chey
Kunla wang gyur thutsal chen
Tsangpey neydang gyamtsoi ling
Gangkar tsedang tsenden nag
Drubpey neyney kurzheng shig

HUNG
In the magnetizing mandala of great bliss,
Enchanter of the minds of all three realms,
Lord Mahadeva and consort,
Endowed with the power to magnetize everyone,
From the abode of Brahma and islands in the ocean,
From white glacier summits and sandalwood jungles,
From the places of sadhana, manifest in your bodily form.

Kudok marpo kalpa yi
Metar barwey zijin gyi
Khamsum malue wangdu due
Chagtsen chagkyu zhagpa yi
Drowey yigug chingwar dzey
Zurphue dawa tsepey gyen
Sangwey tagkyi noechue kyi
Zidang yonten wangdu due

The majestic brilliance of your red body color,
Blazing like the fire of the kalpa,
Takes command over the three realms, without exception.
Your attributes of hook and noose
Captivate and bind the minds of beings.
Your secret sign, the hair tuft adorned with a crescent moon,
Magnetizes magnificent splendor
And all the qualities of the world and beings.

Yumchen lhamo kardok ma
Tagtu chakshing dela rol
Kusung thugkyi kyilkhor ney
Sangwey mazhi leyla gye

Great consort, Goddess Kardokma,༔
Forever passionate and reveling in bliss,༔
From the mandala of your body, speech, and mind,༔
Send forth the four secret ladies to act.༔

Semmey payang gugjey na༔
Yidang denpa moechi goe༔
Tsangdang doekham wangpo sog༔
Drekpey lhachen tamchey kyang༔

Since you magnetize all, even the insentient,༔
It is needless to mention sentient beings,༔
Brahma, the king of the realm of desire, and so forth,༔
And also all the haughty mahadevas.༔

Khyoekyi khordang yoglag tey༔
Jigten sumna draley gyal༔
Kathub drubpa khyoekyi thue༔
Zilgyi minoen gangyang mey༔

These are your retinue and attendants.༔
Thus, you conquer the enemies of the three worlds.༔
By the power of your attainment in ascetic practice,༔
There is no one you fail to dominate.༔

Ngontse zhelzhey damchey pey༔
Thugdam danta kul lagso༔
Khyoekyi thutsal duela bab༔
Gangla jawa khyoekyi shey༔

I now call upon the vow༔
You took and pledged in former times.༔
The time has come for your strength and power.༔
What is to be done is now up to you.༔

Deyi lue ngag yisum la༔
Khyoekyi zhagpey oezhag phong༔
Gugjey chagkyu nyingney drong༔
Sipey lung gi zhagpey ching༔

Catch the body, speech, and mind of the objects,༔
With the noose of your lasso of light.༔

Grip at their hearts with your summoning hook,⁂
And tie them with the rope of the wind of existence.⁂

Rangwang tenpa dangdrel ney⁂
Kechig yuetsam neydi ru⁂
Danta nyidu khugla shog⁂
Gosum khordang longchoe chey⁂
Dag gi wangdu duwar dzoe⁂

Summon those lacking independence and stability,⁂
To come right now,⁂
In a single moment, to this very place.⁂
Bring their body, speech, mind, and enjoyments⁂
Under my command.⁂

Yulri gyalkham gendun dey⁂
Tendzin kyebu gyallon bang⁂
Khyeu phomo drunor sog⁂
Gangsam beymey wangdu due⁂

Valleys, districts, kingdoms, and sanghas,⁂
Masters to uphold the teachings, kings, ministers, and subjects,⁂
Men and women, crops, wealth, and the like,⁂
May whatever I wish for be effortlessly magnetized.⁂

Shatrak zenchen khurwa dang⁂
Poedang metog lasog pa⁂
Tsimpey damdzey kunzhey la⁂
Naljor dagchag khorchey kyi⁂
Barchey solla thunkyen drub⁂

Flesh and blood, rice porridge and honey-molasses,⁂
Incense, flowers, and so forth;⁂
Accept all these satisfying articles of samaya.⁂
For us, the practitioners, and our retinues⁂
Dispel obstacles and provide favorable conditions.⁂

Duela babbo wangchuk che⁂
Phonya drendang ngagpar chey⁂
Duela babbo samaya⁂

The time has arrived, Maheshvara,:
Together with your emissaries, attendants, and messengers.:
The time has arrived, samaya!:

Then offer the torma in a clean place.

By combining a sequence of termas aimed at the particular object of invo-cation, I, Pema Gyurmey, arranged this torma offering to Mahadeva, the guardian of the teachings of the Lotus Dakini within the Seven Profound Teachings, *in the hidden valley of Sikkim. May virtuous goodness increase.*

Ekajati

KURUKULLE EXPLANATION[19]

Tulku Urgyen Rinpoche

The enlightened essence is present in everyone. It is present in every state, both samsara and nirvana, and in all sentient beings—without exception. Experience your buddha nature. Make it your constant practice, and you will reach enlightenment. In my lifetime, I have known many, many people who attained such an enlightened state, both male and female. Awakening to enlightenment is not an ancient fable; it is not mythology. It actually does happen. Bring the oral instructions into your own practical experience, and enlightenment will indeed be possible; it is not merely a fairy tale. Unless you learn how to gain familiarity with your buddha nature, train in it, and realize it, you will remain deluded. Delusion never disappears by itself. Spinning around on the rim of samsara's vicious wheel, on the twelve links of dependent origination, you will continue life after life. We all die, are reborn, and die again—countless times.

But, in this present life, you can learn to recognize your enlightened essence, and if you do that, you can, before passing away, attain the perfect, fully awakened state of a buddha. The sole method for transforming this human body into rainbow light at the moment of death is through realizing buddha nature; there is no other possible way. The teachings for how to do this are still available. Place your trust in the Three Jewels: the precious Buddha, Dharma, and Sangha. Receive this instruction from someone who holds an unbroken lineage. This lineage is still intact. Otherwise, everyone dies; there is no exception. In the past, everyone who lived in this world died. Right now everyone alive will die. Everyone born in the future will also die. Everything in the world changes. Nothing remains the same; nothing is permanent; nothing lasts. If you want to be successful, if you really want to take care of yourself—recognize your enlightened essence.

To realize buddha nature, you need the support of three principles.

---

19 Translated by Erik Pema Kunsang & Marcia B. Schmidt

First is the precious Buddha, the primal teacher who showed the enlightened essence to others. Next is the precious Dharma, the teachings on how to train in experiencing the enlightened essence. Lastly, there is the precious Sangha, the people who uphold and spread the teachings. Additionally, you have the support of the Three Roots: The guru is the root of blessings, the yidam is the root of accomplishment, and the dakini is the root of activities. They possess all-knowing wakefulness, all-embracing compassion, the activity of enacting deeds for the benefit of beings, and the capacity to protect and save others.

The dakinis and protectors are the source of activity, which breaks down into five types: peaceful, increasing, magnetizing, subjugating, and supreme activities. Dakini and protector practices represent the primary way to engage these activities. Among dakinis, wisdom dakinis in space and worldly dakinis are the two principal types. The primary wisdom dakini is the great mother, dharmakaya Samantrabadri. She is like the sun and the different emanations and re-emanations are like the rays of the sun. The sambhogakaya appears as the five space mothers. The nirmanakaya manifests as the five elements. Water is Buddha Mamaki, earth is Buddha Lochana, fire is Buddha Pandaravasini, wind is Buddha Samaya Tara, and space is Buddha Dhatvishvari. Just as these five elements are the five primordial female buddhas, the *skandas* are the five primordial male buddhas.

Meeting the true dakini requires encountering the empty cognizance of your mind. There is cognizance, appearance, bliss, and emptiness. The apparent aspect is the great father, and the empty aspect is the great mother. The doer is Samantrabhadra, and the deed is Samantrabhadri; these two together are the Samantrabhadra great father and mother. They are the root of all of samsara and nirvana.

The dakini expedites the activity, and each treasure revealer receives guidance for how to proceed and gains understanding through the dakinis. The wisdom dakinis and protectors do not come to this human world, so we cannot connect with them. However, they will know whether the yogi has achieved the view and realization. They will find out whether the view has been actualized and perfected. They will see whether or not the yogi has any kind of fixation, hope, or fear. Just as an ordinary, worldly judge watches to see who follows the law or breaks it—and people are rewarded or punished accordingly—likewise, the worldly dakini helps or punishes you according to your view.

If you have attachment to the self and desire benefit for yourself, then you are not a true or real yogi. If you have this, the dakinis will not help but instead will punish you. If you go against your samaya, your realization of the view is mistaken. If you fall on a perverted path of the view and meditation, then you have broken with both the protectors and the dakinis. These dakinis and protectors also pervade the bardo and will make obstacles for you.

There is a story of Patrul Rinpoche that illustrates what happens when a practitioner breaks samaya and how a wisdom dakini can punish him or her. Patrul Rinpoche was at Dodrubchen Monastery, giving teachings on the *Guhyagarbha Tantra*. Jigme Lingpa had two main disciples, Dodrub and Tradrub, and Palgi was a disciple of Tradrub, more commonly known as Gyalwai Nyugyu. Dodrubchen Rinpoche had already passed away when Patrul Rinpoche went to Dodrubchen Monastery in Golok. Initially, Patrul Rinpoche had gone to meet Lama Shabkar, who wrote *The Flight of the Garuda,* but he had passed away before Patrul could meet him. Palgi lamented that he had missed meeting such a great bodhisattva and expressed his own lack of merit and the lack of merit in that place.

Patrul Rinpoche continued on to Dodrubchen Monastery. When he had finished giving the *Guhyagarbha* teachings, he was asked to bestow the reading transmission for the one hundred thousand Nyingma tantras. Before he began the reading, a person who had broken samaya with Dodrubchen Rinpoche arrived, wanting to participate. Breaking samaya with Dodrubchen was like breaking samaya with Gyalwai Nyugyu and Palgi themselves. So Palgi called upon the great dakini Ekajati. In particular, he scolded Ekajati saying, "Aren't you supposed to watch for samaya violators, who break the sacred bond? Like a loving mother, aren't you supposed to be watching out for your children? Where are you looking with that one eye of yours? Are you all of a sudden allowing the samaya corrupters to receive teachings? If so, what is the use of your fang? Why are you behaving like an ignorant old lady? You have no power! You don't even know who keeps and who breaks samayas!" He really chastised her.

That very night, the samaya breaker had a heart attack. He was a famous monk, quite learned, but he died from the heart attack. When Patrul was told that the monk had died, he said, "Oh, your eye has seen and your tooth has benefited. You took care of the samaya breaker. Your activity will expand!" Thus, he praised Ekajati.

Now this monk was lodging at a guesthouse on the monastery grounds, and the owner of the house also got stricken, as a result of staying together with a samaya breaker. Patrul was told about the danger to the life of the guesthouse owner. Once again Palgi scolded Ekajati, "Aren't you supposed to protect the loyal, while liberating violators? Is there something you have misunderstood? You seem to be punishing the innocent. It is reasonable that you liberated the other one, Ekajati; that was your duty as the guardian of the dharmadhatu teachings. But here, you are completely lacking discernment between virtue and crime; it is a huge mistake to hurt the blameless! You must immediately let this man recover. Can't you determine how to act? Don't you know who has no samayas and who needs to suffer the consequences of their karma?" The next morning the sick man was sitting in his place, attending the reading.

Conversely, these wisdom dakinis and protectors will guard you throughout your journey on the paths and bhumis. They escort you from the front, clearing obstacles, and protect you from the back. They are your companions in this life, the bardo, and the next life, assisting you in these three until you reach enlightenment. They are very precious.

The actual text for the outer Kurukulle practice has preliminary, main, and concluding parts. The preliminary here is not like the regular preliminaries you do; it is for this sadhana. It has refuge, bodhichitta, the torma for the obstructors, the protection circle, the rain of blessings, and consecration of offerings. This is a terma of Chokgyur Lingpa, according to the *Profoundity of Longevity* within the *Seven Profound Teachings*. It is an easily applied sadhana, with a comfortable method.[20]

It begins with the lineage prayer, the first of the preliminaries. written by Kongtrül Rinpoche, requesting: *May appearance and mind be magnetized.* Among those to be supplicated are *Lord and Dharma King Trisong Deütsen and son.* The son is Murub Tsenpo, who later incarnated as the treasure revealer Chokgyur Lingpa, possessing the seven transmissions.[21]

The concluding verse states,

> *In the spontaneous and all-pervasive state of primordially free and unchanging self-awareness,*
> *May the expression of awareness, what appears and exists, samsara and nirvana, be magnetized.*
> *Within the single expanse of dharmakaya, the nonduality of appearance and mind,*

May I attain the confidence free from subject and object, effort and cultivation.

One's own rigpa is primordially free. In the expression of rigpa, may whatever appears and exists, samsara and nirvana, be magnetized. *Within the single expanse of dharmakaya* means do not separate appearance as over there and mind as here. Appearance and mind are the single sphere of dharmakaya. Finally, you are making aspirations to attain the confidence free from subject and object, doer and deed. May all duality be mingled into one taste, beyond effort and cultivation.

When beginning a Kurukulle retreat, it is necessary to offer a white torma, *kartor,* when you go to a very wild place, where practice has not been engaged in before. However, if you are living in Nepal or India, where the land is already subjugated, you can dispense with this. In Nepal and India, the ground has been consecrated by many buddhas and bodhisattvas, who have tamed the local spirits, so these divinities hold no resentment against practitioners. On the contrary, they have no envy. Yet it can happen that if you go to a completely new place, the spirits of the land will feel jealous of your practicing; they won't like it. Therefore, it is important to give a white torma. It's just like paying rent for the house where you reside. You make two offerings: First, you give to the spirit of the country and then to the spirit of the locale.

The refuge and bodhichitta come from the terma text, this is the second part of the preliminaries. The condensation of the identity of all buddhas is the lama and the dakini. The noble sangha provides benefit for both studying and practicing the dharma. Monasteries, and the ordained sangha who stay in them, are important sources of support. Without such a place, the sangha could not come together and be sustained. In India, the Buddha did not have a monastery, but three major monasteries originated from him: the temple at the stupa of enlightenment in Bodhgaya, Nalanda Monastery, and Vikramashila Monastery. Each had five hundred panditas, very large gatherings. When speaking about the monastery here, it refers to Samye in Tibet, where Padmasambhava and Vimalamitra were. Samye had khenpos and lopons—one hundred and eight altogether came from India. Of course, the main ones were Padmasambhava and Vimalamitra.

And produce all the necessities for Dharma practice, means to make a monastery and house the sangha. *I pledge to accomplish the guru dakini* refers to the dakini and Padmasambhava. *So, without any difficulty, may I achieve this right now.* That line is expressing the bodhichitta, the reasons for accomplishing the Dharma. You recite this refuge and bodhichitta three times.

This is the purpose of practicing the Padma Dakini and enacting magnetizing activity. Usually the four activities and the eight general accomplishments belong to the relative or common siddhis. The four activities are pacifying, increasing, magnetizing, and subjugating. The eight general or common accomplishments are the invisibility, the sword, the ability to find subterranean treasure, and so forth. There are eight feats that can be accomplished. In this particular case, there is a slight difference because Kurukulle is, in essence, Vajravarahi, who is a wisdom dakini, not a mundane deity. Vajravarahi only assumes a form for those who want to accomplish the magnetizing activity for a definite reason. The reason is to magnetize kings, ministers, merchants, men, women, wealth, medicines, and so forth.

What is the real purpose of doing magnetizing practice? The real essence that needs to be magnetized is not these superficial things. We need to magnetize realization of the view, thus, the teachings on how to realize the view, meditation, and conduct. *Meditation* refers to those who do practice, and *conduct* refers to those who act in accordance with the Vinaya and so forth. Basically, a primary purpose of magnetizing activity is to sustain the sangha of Buddhist practitioners. We have no mundane purpose for magnetizing wealth, influence, or power; we use it only to sustain Buddhism.

If you are totally poor, you will have no way to sustain a monastery and a great gathering of monks to continue the Buddhadharma. Milarepa was a very accomplished and realized practitioner, but if you live alone in the mountains, as he did, you will have no one to build a huge temple and provide food for a large congregation. It's very important in the current age to magnetize sponsors, wealth, influential patrons, and so forth to allow for things to happen.

Among the four or six different periods of the Buddha's teaching, we are now in the last period, called *taktsam dzinpa,* upholding the mere externals or merely the signs. This means that the main way to benefit beings and practitioners is to simply keep up the image of being Buddhist practitioners; this is all you can do these days. It's not like the time of the Buddha, which was the period of accomplishment. In this day and age, it is extremely important to maintain big impressive monasteries. Funds are needed in order to build and maintain them, so you need to magnetize the funds, the influence to build them, the practitioners, benefactors, and so on. Even if there are only a few monks or nuns, as few as four or even just two, there are still incredibly great blessings for everyone involved. Yet, it definitely requires funds. As a single individual, you may not be able to accomplish such an enormous endeavor, but the Buddha said that just having the concern that the Dharma will die out has incredibly great merit, even if you cannot sustain the whole sangha. So, the whole purpose of magnetizing activity is to gather the positive conditions for the Buddha-dharma to continue.

The next section of the text is the torma for the two types of obstructing forces, physical enemies who are embodied and obstructors who have no substantiality and cannot be seen, the third preliminary. Offering the *gektor* is like giving a bribe where you say, "I'm trying to accomplish the state of enlightenment. Please don't obstruct me. Take this torma and get out!" There are three ways to give them a torma: You can first offer in a peaceful way, expressing, "Best you go." Then you can become more insistent, and finally you can become wrathful, reciting wrathful mantras. You imagine yourself as Padma Heruka, in whose heart center is the syllable HRING. Padma Heruka is primarily Tamdrin, *Who has mastered all of samsara and nirvana*, as the sadhana states. You should think, "I have control over all of samsara and nirvana. There is nothing that is out of my control. My command is the vajra command, do not transgress it!" *Disperse into innate space* means that when thoughts are freed, then liberation, the state of buddhahood, and everything in between, [are] *primordially empty and rootless*. Primordially, everything is empty, like space, which has no root, no source. In a mundane way, you apply intelligence through the three methods of being peaceful, insistent, and wrathful. If that does not work then you send them away from within the view, the expanse of primordial purity.

Next, draw the boundary for protection, which is the fourth. *Sights, sounds, and thoughts are deity, mantra, and the space of luminosity*. Sights are the deities, sound is the mantra, and all thoughts are the primordially pure space of luminosity. The protection circle is *filled with rainbow rays, attributes, and a blazing mass of fire*.

This is followed by the gesture of homage, confession, and taking the oath, the fifth. To begin, offer prostrations, and then, confess, to repair damaged samayas. Taking the oath is acknowledging that you and the deity are inseparable. This is the true samaya. Opening the door of means and knowledge indicates that these are the doors to encountering your own awareness as the deity. Neither means nor knowledge can be abandoned; if they are, you will not meet the deity. Means and knowledge are always united, from the Shravaka path up until complete enlightenment. For the shravakas, this unity is emptiness and compassion; for Vajrayana, it is development and completion stages, and for Dzogchen, it is primordially pure Trekchö and spontaneously present Tögal. I pay the ultimate homage of realizing nonduality beyond concepts. Beyond concepts means "nondual." To ultimately realize the view is the homage. I confess my confused fixation on separateness: Here, you confess having fallen into confusion, thinking that self and other exist and fixating on these differentiations. This confession is beyond fixating. And vow to keep the vajra oath of constant practice. This line indicates you are not separate from emptiness-awareness wisdom, the vajra oath, which is beyond concepts. The root of all samayas is the unchanging vajra, emptiness. You pledge to keep that samaya. vajra samaya hung. The heart syllable of all buddhas is hung.

Sixth is bringing down the great resplendence of wisdom. In the preliminaries, you bring down the blessings of everything that appears and exists—from the outer vessel and the celestial palace to the inner contents and the nature of the deity. HRIH *From the shining palace of magnetizing great bliss* is the red crescent with a single door. *Gurus of the three lineages, peaceful and wrathful yidam deities* refers to the mind lineage of the victorious ones, the symbolic lineage of the vidyadharas, and individual hearing lineage as well as the peaceful and wrathful yidams. *Dakinis of the three abodes* refers to the abode of the body of rainbow light, the abode of the seven profundities of speech, and the deep abode of mind. *Dharma protectors possessing the samaya*: this phrase indicates the sixty-four holy places of Chakrasamvara and the sixty-four holy places of dakas. *And especially Padma Dakini, chief figure, and entourage*: The main figures in the padma family are Amitayus, Avalokiteshvara, and Padmasambhava—and when wrathful, Tamdrin and Padma Heruka; all of these are being referred to here. When Avalokiteshvara has a consort, she is Sangwa Yeshe, essentially the same as Padma Dakini.

With great yearning means that the hairs of your body stand on edge and tears flow from your eyes. *I call upon you* means you call out with such intensity, *Invoking your promise,* to all you wisdom deities dwelling in space, while beating the damaru with faith and devotion. You are requesting the deities to please *bestow a great resplendence upon this site of sadhana.* Come here to this place, Padma Khandro and retinue, and *Confer the great empowerment upon me, a yogi of the supreme sadhana.* The yogi is asking for the empowerments of body, speech, and mind and all three together, which is the precious word empowerment. *Consecrate the articles of sadhana as wisdom forms.* The articles of sadhana are not ordinary, worldy substances but wisdom substances. Here you are asking for blessings for the unconditional substances.

May sights and sounds, all phenomena, come under the sway of awareness. Sights, sounds, and awareness are not over there; they come under the sway of awareness. *May samsara and nirvana be perfected as the great sphere of equality.* Samsara and nirvana are not divided; they are the great equality, the single sphere of dharmakaya. *Within this primordially*—it is this way from the beginning; it is not temporary; it is the *unchanging state of luminous great bliss. May you bestow the resplendence of the great, all-encompassing spontaneous perfection.* Spontaneous presence and spontaneous perfection are the same, and they are all-encompassing like space, with no center or edge. Please bestow this resplendence. VAJRA JNANA ABESHAYA A AH. Please quickly do this! This was the section on bringing down the resplendence.

The seventh section is consecrating the offerings, from the terma root text. OM VAJRA AMRITA KUNDALI HUNG PHAT is the wrathful mantra for sprinkling. Cleanse with RAM YAM KHAM and purify with OM SOBHAVA (and so forth). *Within the state of emptiness appears a shining lotus vessel.* From OM AH HUNG, *the different types of offerings* emerge. Outwardly, these include the seven types of offerings; inwardly, amrita, rakta, and torma; secretly, union, liberation, emptiness, and the absolute offering. *Are individually manifest as a cloud of wisdom offerings, Appearing in potent forms that generate bliss, fascinate, and magnetize.* Bliss is mahasukha, which your own mind generates. *Appearing as potent forms* indicates these dharma materials have power and are individually manifest like stars in the sky. Many appear, not merely one, and they turn into both benefit and harm. OM AH HUNG is the blessing of body, speech, and mind. VAJRA SAPHARANA KHAM means bless all the offerings. *By uttering this mantra three times, Consecrate the offerings and enter the actual sadhana.* Please give accomplishment.

This Padma Dakini preliminary precedes the practice. It is not like the four hundred thousand preliminary practices; it is the supreme preliminary for this sadhana. In accord with the wish of the supreme Choying, The Nirmanakaya of Palnge, this was written by Chimey Tennyi Lingpa, Kongtrül Rinpoche. There are two kinds of Bonpos, white and black ones. Kongtrül Rinpoche was a white one, who had the name Bonpo but was a pure bendi, or monk. He appeared out of the kindness of Padmasambhava and was a true treasure revealer called Tennyi Lingpa, who came to benefit both doctrines. Directly as it came to mind. By the virtue of this may personal experience be brought under control. Once you gain mastery over your own experience, you can do so with others. If you are unable to control your own personal experience, there is no way to magnetize others. Once you have tamed your own mind, your experience, then naturally you will gain the power to control others. May virtuous goodness increase.

Now for the commentary on the main body of the sadhana of the Lotus Dakini for Magnetizing Activity.

Sadhana practice has the three aspects: approach, accomplishment, and enacting the activities. This is a practice for enacting the activities, according to the *Profundity of Longevity* within the *Seven Profound Treasures*. It begins with two dakini scripts that Padmasambhava first revealed. An intellectual cannot understand these; each symbol of the dakini script is the size of a country, like Nepal, for example. Within this, the small letters clearly show what the dakini script emanates. Enlightened body, speech, and mind are complete within them.

The first line starts with: *I, Padma, who devotedly bows down to the mother of the victorious ones.* This references the great dharmakaya mother, to whom he pays homage. Padmasambhava then states that he *Will teach the sadhana of the Lotus Dakini for magnetizing activity.* Among the four activities, peaceful, increasing, magnetizing, and subjugating, this practice is meant for the magnetizing activity. *In order to benefit future upholders of the teachings* refers to the great ones who disseminate the teachings. During the Dark Age, if there are no lamas or monks who can uphold the doctrine, it will degenerate. As I mentioned earlier, merely worrying that the doctrine will decline has immense merit.

First, go to a secluded place,

Which should have red soil and cliffs or rocks with sharp edges.

Draw a crescent-shaped mandala with a perfect door in the center,

With an enclosure of lotus flowers, vajras, and flames of fire.

In the middle, draw an eight-petaled flower, and in its center,

Draw a red lotus flower marked with hooks.

To do this practice, choose a secluded place that has red soil. Use sindura to draw the crescent-shaped mandala. Then put wine inside a copper vase. Gather the three magnetizing substances: a magnet, which is the primary ingredient; red flowers that have pistils shaped like hooks; and coral. You can use lama medicine, because that has all the different substances and nectars. Just follow the instructions in the small writing at the beginning of the text. The torma needs to have the "juice" of wine, *should be adorned with butter-flowers and red hooks* and *formed by the hands of a beautiful girl,* who has an attractive face and is from a good class. If you can do that, it is very good. *Sprinkle fragrant ointment on this cubit-sized torma. Beautify eight similar types with a canopy of red silk.* These represent the retinue of eight Kurukulles who enact the activities.

Moreover, mentally create and arrange similar articles, As well as the outer, inner, and secret offerings. You, yourself, should wear red ornaments, garlands, and clothing. You as the practitioner need to wear red clothing and have a red mala as well as red ornaments. Regarding the different criteria for this practice, it's best to follow exactly what it says; you can ask for help from others. You can do the elaborate version, if you like, but if you prefer the simple version, it is fine to just imagine that all these things are present. That's the style of the *Namchö,* Mingyur Dorje's termas. All of them say you can just visualize the tormas, the mandala, and so forth: *Within the sky of primordial purity, the clouds of offerings appear.* It's like that. To practice without a mandala, or torma, and so forth is fine. Just do the best you can, however it feels most convenient.

After imagining all the victorious ones present in the sky before you, take refuge here, if you did not already do so in the previously explained preliminaries. Now comes the main part, wherein the three samadhis purify all clinging to solidity. They purify all thoughts, such as holding to earth as earth, fire as fire, and water as water.

The most important aspect here is the view of Trekchö. You should chant while remaining in the view of Trekchö. Then, sometimes, you can imagine the hooks pulling things in and bringing them under your control; there will be some benefit this way. However, if you just sit and send out hooks in a dualistic way, bringing things from there to here without the view of Trekchö, you will not attain much accomplishment. Conceptual thoughts cannot magnetize; it's the nonconceptual view of wisdom that magnetizes. If normal thinking were enough, there would be no point in doing a practice, because ordinary craving would achieve accomplishment. Since this is not the case, you need deity, mantra, and samadhi, all three. If you have all three complete, it is possible to magnetize what needs to be magnetized.

You just think, "I'm Kurukulle." Then repeat the mantra. While remaining in the state of the view, let the rays of light take the form of hooks and gather what should be brought back. You're not merely putting hooks in people. You are mingling their state of mind and your state of mind, which is the continuity of the view, so they become identical. If you don't dissolve them indivisibly, you can pull them in, but then they slip away again. They sneak out. What are you going to do if they sneak out? You bring them under control and magnetize both material and ethereal beings.

In a simple practitioner's case, you should focus more on the supreme accomplishments, not the common ones. In order to attain supreme accomplishment, you need to have an unmistaken view, meditation, and conduct. To achieve these three, Padma Dakini practice is incredibly beneficial.

Kurukulle is none other than the Padma Dakini. Sakya Pandita practiced her his entire life, but the accomplishment did not appear for him. It did manifest for his nephew, who then became the personal guru of the Chinese emperor and gained control over the entire country of Tibet. The Chinese emperor and Chögyal Phakpa Rinpoche were renowned as the "benefactor and guru." They were famous, and it was said that in the heavens, there are two, the sun and the moon; on the earth, there are two, the patron and officiating priest.

So, if you don't gain accomplishment from the practice in this lifetime, it will certainly come through in the next life. (Rinpoche laughs.) This is a very profound practice. Padma Dakini is surrounded by eight other dakinis who, in fact, carry out the four activities. Padma Dakini is like the queen or empress, while the surrounding dakinis are like the emissaries or ministers, who accomplish all four activities. In this practice, you need not be concerned with facing any particular direction or choosing the right time of day. Only the fire puja offering[22] specifies a certain time of day to practice, a direction to face, and a sitting position to assume for each of the four activities. For example, this is the wrathful position, whereby you sit like this, so you can heave the hammer or other weapons.

There is also a certain attitude to adopt. For example, the pacifying activity requires a very gentle, peaceful attitude while you put the things in the fire, recite the chants, and so on. The increasing activity calls for a very generous, magnanimous attitude, as though you already possess everything. The magnetizing activity necessitates the attitude that you already control everything. The subjugating activity requires the attitude of smashing everything into dust. These different attitudes are not really dualistic in nature. While remaining in the view, you flavor it with a certain attitude, while never actually leaving the samadhi behind. When you read in the different sutras that the Buddha entered this and that samadhi, understand that he flavored the state of self-existing wakefulness (*rangjung yeshe*) with a certain mood. There are not really different types of samadhis, but more like different shades.

The principal mood of Kurukulle is passionate. I assume you know the meaning of "passionate," but you should not take this in a dualistic, worldly sense. Rather, while you are in the view of self-existing wakefulness, have a passionate attitude or flavor to it. This is very important when doing the practice.

Finally, the conclusion of the daily sadhana is at the end of the feast. It's all right not to do the feast offering every day, so just jump to what comes after the feast.

MAGNETIZING PRACTICE[23]

Orgyen Tobgyal Rinpoche

When you receive an empowerment, it is necessary to do the practice for that empowerment. The lineage empowerment is first, followed by the path empowerments, which altogether authorize disciples to do the practices. The path vase empowerment is for the practice of the development stage. The path secret empowerment is for the practices of channels, winds, and essences as well as mantra recitation. The path wisdom-knowledgment empowerment utilizes the emptiness of the example wisdom to encourage the ultimate wisdom being to arise in your experience. The secret and the wisdom-knowledge empowerments correspond to completion stage with and without characteristics, respectively. The precious word empowerment authorizes you to practice Dzogchen, primordially pure Trekchö and spontaneously present Tögal. The best disciples will maintain an unbroken flow. Immediately upon receiving this empowerment, they will instantly be undeluded, undistracted, and practice the path. The middling ones can maintain awareness six times in a day. Those with lesser capacity will hold this awareness at least one time each day. This is the process of receiving the four empowerments for yidam practice. You must practice until you truly actualize the result of the path, without breaking the continuity of the deity.

After you receive the lineage empowerment, utilize the deity empowerment and do not abandon sadhana practice. If you practice the deity after receiving the lineage empowerment, you will ultimately become enlightened and temporarily receive the fruition empowerment. The fruition empowerment bestows all the qualities of the three kayas of buddhahood. At that point, you will effortlessly benefit innumerable sentient beings as vast as the sky. I have given this condensed explanation of empowerment so you can understand. Merely receiving empower-

---

23 Translated by Gyurme Avertin & Marcia B. Schmidt

ment from a lama has a bit of benefit, but without practicing, you will not become enlightened.

ENHANCEMENT

With the vase empowerment, you recite the mantras for the outer, inner, and secret practices. You visualize the deity and maintain that visualization with vivid presence. Once you have accumulated the appropriate numbers, you should have made a connection with the practice. Jamgön Kongtrül Rinpoche wrote a commentary on how to do retreat on Kurukulle, which you can follow if you want to do a retreat.

Anyway, if you have made a connection with the vase empowerment, everything you see with your eyes can be magnetized or brought under control.[24] You do that by thinking, "I am Padma Khandro." Visualize that clearly. You can engage in the enhancement for this by meditating on a red syllable OM in each of your eyes. As these red OM syllables radiate light, the wisdom of great bliss blazes supremely. The blazing light from your eyes pervades all appearances. This light radiates outwardly, clearly illuminating everything it touches, like the light from the sun. All appearances become the light of great bliss, which flows back into the OM syllables in your eyes. The outer objects and the inner subject are magnetized inseparably. The eyes bring all forms under control.

In order to bring all sounds under control, imagine that red SHANG syllables are in your ears. As before, red light rays of great bliss radiate outwardly from the SHANG syllables. They permeate all sounds, which become light and dissolve back into the SHANG syllables in the ears; all sounds are magnetized. Similarly, from the nasal scepter, red KHAM syllables radiate red light rays of great bliss that permeate all smells. Once touched by this light, the smells are transformed into the light of great bliss, which returns and dissolves into the KHAM syllables in the nose specter. All smells are magnetized or brought under control. In the same way on the tongue, a red RAM syllable sends out red light rays of great bliss that reach all the different tastes, sweet and sour. Again they melt into light and the red light returns and dissolves into the RAM on your tongue, whereby all tastes are brought under control or magnetized. In the forehead, a red SUM sends out light rays of great bliss that reach all the tactile sensations, which become red light permeated with great bliss.

This light returns to dissolve into the red SUM syllable in the forehead. In the middle of the heart is a red HANG syllable. Red light of great bliss blazes forth from this HANG, permeating all mental fixation on phenomena. All appearances dissolve into the red light, which reabsorbs into the HANG syllable in your heart.

These are the six syllables pertaining to sensorial objects and mental phenomena. If you meditate on these gradually and sequentially, the objects of all six consciousnesses and the subject, the six consciousnesses themselves, will become one taste, and you will gain mastery over them.

Meditating like this, you will attain the fruition, realizing that all appearances, sounds, smells, tastes, and touchables are empty. Furthermore, you will realize that all knowables, all mental phenomena, are empty bliss. The two truths are indivisible, and you will remain in a state of experiencing all as illusory. At the same time that you visualize the syllables, you also chant each of them.

Do this practice to gain powerful mastery over all the appearances of the six consciousnesses. Sometimes think of yourself as Kurukulle, without a consort in the outer and inner practices and with consort Lokeshvara in the secret practice. Visualize the yab and yum with vivid presence. Like the deity dissolving into the deity, all appearances dissolve into the deity, and you develop stable pride. When you gain control over appearances, you have received the vase empowerment.

Think about these teachings. First, to practice this, you need to have clear visualization, vivid presence, and pure recollection of Padma Khandro. Otherwise, you will not be able to follow this path. Once you are able to clearly visualize yourself as Padma Khandro with stable pride, then you can continue on to reciting the syllables, starting with OM in the eyes. Om radiates rays of light, permeating all forms. The light rays dissolve into the forms, which become red light, and that light slowly merges back into the OM syllables in your eyes. Once they dissolve, you gain control over all forms, which are sealed with emptiness. Then you continue with the visualizations for the other five consciousnesses. This is how to train. During this practice, you need to maintain the clear visualization of yourself as the deity and not separate from that.

In short, the main aspect of the vase empowerment is developing the deity. The second empowerment is connected to Anuyoga's practices with the channels, winds, and essence. The last two empowerments relate to Atiyoga. Having received the empowerment of Padma Khandro, you need to keep these ordinary and extraordinary samayas: Treat women with the greatest respect and kindness, maintain the mudra and mantra recitation uninterruptedly, and do the practice. Just receiving an empowerment and listening to teachings are not the most important things. The most vital is to practice and accomplish what you receive. Once you follow the Vajrayana path—where you receive empowerments and teachings and practice development and completion—it will not be long before you attain the state of buddhahood. Practice is essential.

One important element of practice is the tradition of the great accomplishment, drubchen. In *Lama Gongdu*, Padmasambhava said that one week of drubchen practice is the same as seven years of retreat. When you perform a drubchen, the life force of the sadhana is the mantra. Through the recitation, you connect to the wisdom mind of the deity, enabling you to receive the blessings and accomplishments. In a drubchen, the recitation is unbroken. There is power in the great accomplishment practice.

APPLICATION

This Kurukulle cycle has sadhanas for outer, inner, and secret practices, and each of these has a different visualization and recitation. This cycle also contains a Three Roots practice, and the Kurukulle practice is a branch of this. In the outer practice, you meditate on yourself as Padma Khandro, who has a retinue of eight dakinis that are exactly the same as she is. At the four doors, there are another four female gatekeepers.

In Vajrayana, you need to think about the meaning of the words you recite and meditate on them. You can easily do the short daily practice and recite the mantra, which is the wisdom mind of the deity. The daily practice begins with taking refuge, generating bodhichitta, and reciting the Seven-Branch prayer. Based on the three samadhis, you instantaneously visualize yourself as the deity. It is good to have a photo of the deity as a samaya support for your self-visualization. Based on this samaya support, you visualize yourself as the deity and think that you are one and the same, which will give rise to seven experiences, as it is said in the tantras.

Buddha nature is present in all sentient beings. The ultimate point of Vajrayana is to ascertain that all phenomena have the nature of the three kayas. It is not a question of your being inadequate; it is only a matter of not realizing this view. Habitual tendencies obscure this view, and in order to train in purifying them, you must practice deity yoga. To accomplish a deity, you need to know that it does not come from outside of yourself. When realizing this view, you authentically accomplish the deity; therefore, practice sadhana.

Meditating on a deity requires vivid presence, seeing all the different attributes, down to the white and black of the eyes, as images reflected in a mirror. There is nothing the mind is not capable of thinking. Our core, the buddha nature, is pure and the deity is pure. You need to give up the discursive thinking that the deity is good and you are bad and that you need to accomplish the [outer] deity. *Stable* means it is not something you need to conjure up, as though it didn't already exist. Stable pride is knowing *what is* to be *as it is*.

Pure recollection is knowing that, ultimately, you and the deity and the mantra to be accomplished are the expression of emptiness. These come from nowhere else, and in the essence of emptiness, there is nothing. However, to say everything is emptiness is not that easy to explain. Since many of you have received pith instructions on Dzogchen, this is training in rigpa that has been introduced. In short, sometimes train in pure recollection, sometimes in stable pride, and sometimes in vivid presence. When pure recollection has dissolved, train in the empty aspect. Practice all three of these indivisibly.

This is how to practice the development of a deity. For the practice of the enlightened speech of the mantra recitation, follow the daily practice. The mind accomplishes the enlightened body and speech. If you can remain in the nonconceptual samadhi, you will accomplish the completion stage of enlightened mind. If a yogi practices the vajra body, speech, and mind of the deity, the impure aspects of ordinary body, speech, and mind become purified, the purity wisdom is realized, and the enlightened body, speech, and mind are actualized. Truly, you transform into the vajra body, speech, and mind, and the qualities and activities are spontaneously accomplished. This is how you are going to try to practice with your body, speech, and mind. Whatever I have explained is in accordance with the oral instructions of the vidyadharas. Studying and hearing teachings are a lamp for clearing away ignorance, so understanding is a vital point. Nonpractitioners do not need to receive teachings.

Four Doors

A crucial point in Vajrayana is the four doors of Secret Mantra. The first of these is the ultimate clarification based on the "door of words." This door refers to the sadhanas, the means of accomplishment, which remind you of the ultimate essence, the basic state. This is the first of the four doors to be entered. Entering and realizing the ultimate clarification relies on your doing the sadhana from beginning to end, from refuge through the aspirations, with each word reminding you of the meaning.

In the recitation and meditation of the Secret Mantra, you recite the words with your mouth and meditate on the meaning with your mind. The crucial meaning of the words is the mudra of the vidyadhara lineage. Slowly, you sing the melodies and tunes. The benefit of repeating the words and thinking about the meaning is that after a long time you grow accustomed to them. My hope is that you will be able to enter this door. With sadhanas, it does not matter how elaborate or short they are; the ultimate meaning is mostly the same. So, this is the first door.

The second door is the heart-vow, the sacred pledge of the recitation, the "door of the mantra." What is that heart-vow? It is that you and the deity are not separate. You are not accomplishing something better than you. The heart-vow, the sacred pledge, equalizes you and the deity. There are the three recitation intents: approach, accomplishment, and the activities. Once you enter this door, you accumulate the mantra.

The third is the "door of the one-pointed mental visualization samadhi." Through concentration, you need to maintain the samadhi of the visualization. This relates to the essential point of pith instructions of the four nails or the four stakes²⁵ that bind the life force of the practice. These teachings are extremely important, and if you do not know these four stakes, then you do not know the condensed, crucial points. The final stake is that of the unchanging wisdom mind. So, this is the third door.

Lastly, you have the "door of the mudra of what needs to be done." At the time of meditating on the deity, visualize the three doors sealed by the three vajras and yourself crowned by the victorious ones. Invite the wisdom beings and make offerings and praises. All of these are the door of the mudra of what needs to be done.

These correspond to the tantras' references to deity, mantra, samadhi, and mudra. If even one of these four doors is missing, they are incomplete. In Vajrayana, if you practice the development of Mahayoga, then during great accomplishment, you need to enter these four doors. Once you enter the four doors, you will see the precious wheel of the mandala. These four are extremely important.

Since beginingless time up until now, sentient beings have been wandering in samsara. The vital point is that we have not examined our minds. Why have we not examined our minds? Buddha nature pervades all sentient beings; the mind is buddha. However, the essence of buddhahood has been obscured by inexhaustible thoughts, like the ripples on the surface of water. The thoughts arising likes ripples on water are endless. For hundreds of thousands of lifetimes, we have not been able to end thoughts. So how do we reach the point of ending them? We do that through the pith instructions of a lama, which direct you to investigate your mind. The teachings that show you how to examine your mind are the beginning of the end of thoughts.

One way to end thoughts is to employ them, by visualizing the deity, reciting the mantra, and remaining in samadhi. You have received the empowerment, [are trying to] maintain the samaya, and are training in deity yoga. At the time of practice, keep your body, speech, and mind focused one-pointedly. Concerning body, speech, and mind, the main one is the mind, which needs to be undistracted. If you just keep your mind in an ordinary way, following after different thoughts, you are distracted. According to Mahayoga, *nondistraction* means clearly visualizing the deity. Doing this destroys ordinary thoughts. Once you destroy ordinary thoughts by developing this vivid presence, then you train in the vajra pride, thinking, "I am the deity." When vajra pride arises within your stream-of-being, you recognize the buddha nature, the ground of buddha; thus, you have empowered yourself. At the end of your practice with vivid presence and stable pride, you will obtain the blessings of the deity. *Obtaining blessings* means that ordinary thoughts have ceased; there is only the purity of the deity and the display of wisdom, and these are the blessings. When your own appearances are pure and you no longer have any impure experience, you can slowly bring others under control. With these three, all appearances become the form of Padma Khandro. If you have visualized clearly and hold the stable pride of being the magnetizing deity Padma Khandro, it truly becomes so. On the basis of these, you achieve blessings. Then thoughts of the three times, past, present, and future, become like drawings on water. They dissolve into basic space and are liberated, wherein you gain mastery or control over your mind. All thoughts are naturally purified, and you attain the blessings and the power, or strength. To increase the strength of the blessings within this samadhi, recite the mantra. When the samadhi is like a fire, the recitation is like the wind. When the fire of samadhi blazes, the wind makes the fire even greater. Similarly, to increase the samadhi, recite the mantra.

RECITATION

Your recitation should not be either too loud or too soft; your chanting should be heard by you own ear. Pronounce each syllable clearly and sometimes sing the mantra. This singing increases the power of samadhi and the offerings. The lamas, yidams, and dakinis are pleased, and evil deeds and obscurations are purified. Like that, the four activities of the four recitations are accomplished, and the male and female protectors are enjoined. For the practitioner of Dzogchen, all forms of the deity and all thoughts that arise are not beyond primordial purity. Maintaining that awareness decisively renders deity, mantra, samadhi, and mudra the display of dharmakaya. Just remaining like that is the meditation and this is all right.

There are nine aspects of mantra recitation that are common to all mantras. The deity and the mantra are not separate; they are the same. Be certain of that and decide on it. Know that the recitation of the mantra accomplishes the deity. The first aspect is to know the deity and the mantra to be the same.

In reciting one mantra of OM KURU KULLE HRIH SOHA, you can accomplish the mandalas of all the victorious ones. The second aspect is to know the mantra to be the mandala of the victorious ones. The recitation of the mantra, the lights emanating and reabsorbing, and the offerings bring the mandalas of all the victorious ones closer. The third aspect is to know the mantra to be the offering garland.

By reciting the mantra, you accomplish experience, realization, wisdom, and all blessings. The fourth aspect is to know the mantra to be the blessings. In the recitation of the mantra, you can accomplish the supreme siddhi, buddhahood. You can obtain the common and supreme siddhis, all the enlightened activities, and the eight accomplishments. The fifth aspect is to know the mantra to be the siddhis.

Mantra recitation accomplishes infinite activities, including the peaceful, increasing, magnetizing, and subjugating activities as well as power and long life without sickness. The sixth aspect is to know the mantra to be the activities. For example, when someone recites a mantra and blows on a sick person or blows on water, the sick person can be healed by receiving that breath or drinking that water.

Fixation on solid reality can be destroyed and emptiness can be realized by reciting the mantra. The seventh aspect is to know that the mantra reveals emptiness. Simply by reciting AH you can come to realize emptiness. In the recitation of mantra, all breakages, obscurations, and evil deeds can be purified from the root. The eighth aspect is to know the mantra to be purification. By reciting the mantra, all wishes are accomplished. It is like a wish-fulfilling jewel. When a Buddhist supplicates a wish-fulfilling jewel, everything desired is granted. I am not sure that these exist today, but reciting the mantra can accomplish all things. The power of mantra is inconceivable. The ninth is to know the mantra to be a wish-fulfilling jewel.

Since in a drubchen [or a sadhana], you will recite many mantras, it is good to know the ultimate meaning of mantra. Otherwise, just sitting there with your eyes closed and accumulating mantras, without knowing what you have said, will have no benefit. On the other hand, knowing this and reciting with the correct visualization, you will derive great benefit. It is important to understand and repeatedly remind yourself of the meaning. As it is said, when you practice Secret Mantrayana, and in particular the profound treasure dharma [terma], these practices are easily applied with little hardship and great benefit.

The visualization for the recitation of this activity practice is as stated in the text, and I will talk more about that later. The activity is to magnetize, and it is up to each one of you to decide what or who you want to magnetize. There are three kinds of beings: nagas, spirits, and humans—and there are many different types of humans.

> *Through respect and devotion, magnetize a master.*
> *Through swift learning and reflection, magnetize the sacred Dharma.*
> *Through carefulness, magnetize the three gates.*
> *Through compassion, magnetize all sentient beings.*
> *Through a mudra, magnetize my own mind.*
> *Through great bliss, magnetize primordial wakefulness.*

Through primordial wakefulness, magnetize all the victorious ones.⸙

Through blessings, magnetize the dharma protectors.⸙

Through the expression of awareness, magnetize all that appears and exists.⸙

Through majestic splendor, magnetize kingly rulers.⸙

Through samaya, magnetize the dakinis.⸙

Through renown, magnetize all countries.⸙

For the benefit of the teachings, magnetize the Mahayana sangha.⸙

For the benefit of beings, magnetize gods, nagas, and humans.⸙

For the benefit of affluence, magnetize food, clothing, and wealth.⸙

For the benefit of dominion, magnetize attendants, disciples, and followers.⸙

Magnetize harmonious companions, fame, and abundance.⸙

In short, magnetize all the splendor of samsaric existence and nirvanic peace.⸙

To accomplish Padma Khandro, you need devotion. If you have devotion, you can magnetize the lama. If you magnetize the lama, then you will receive all the blessings. If you are practicing Padma Khandro, your great intelligence will expand. Having magnetized the learned and accomplished teacher, you will receive many instructions, and through listening and reflecting, your learning and contemplating will increase. Through learning and reflection, you magnetize the sacred Dharma.

If you practice Padma Khandro, your mind will become more relaxed and careful. If you mind is careful, you will bring your three doors of body, speech, and mind under control. You will refrain from doing or saying things you shouldn't. You will have no need to be thoughtless.

If you practice Padma Khandro, great compassion will naturally arise, and everyone will like you. People do not like someone who lacks compassion, even if it's a lama.

Magnetizing through a mudra refers to taking a consort. To increase wisdom of the ultimate meaning in your stream-of-being, in order to bring your own mind under control, you need to take support of the wisdom mudra. This gives birth to the wisdom of great bliss. If the wisdom of great bliss arises, then the wisdom of ultimate meaning ensues, based on the example of great-bliss wisdom. If this [is a correct experience of] wakefulness, you accomplish all the victorious ones and all the yidams. If you accomplish all the victorious ones, by their blessings, you accomplish all the protectors.

The victorious ones are not deluded. All of mind's different discursive thoughts are the expression, or display, of dharmakaya awareness. If you decide that there is nothing other than the display of the dharmakaya, then you gain control of all that appears and exists. And if you gain control of all that appears and exists, then you become Padmasambhava. If you do not achieve this, but gain control over yourself, it is a bit good and you will magnetize kings and presidents.

By practicing Padma Khandro, you amend your samayas, especially all broken samayas with the dakinis. If your samayas are pure, naturally, you will magnetize the dakinis.

When you practice Padma Khandro, you become famous, for better or worse. Once famous, you magnetize all countries. When a famous person comes out with a new movie, we flock to it. Becoming famous is a big pursuit these days, with advertising, Internet, movies, magazines, and books. Any fame that you garner should be for the benefit of the teachings, magnetizing Mahayana practitioners.

To benefit sentient beings, magnetize gods, nagas, and humans. Never magnetize to harm, but only to benefit. The best benefit is to bring beings to the Dharma. If the Vajrayana practitioner does not have any means, it is difficult to do anything. Even for the sambhogakaya in the Akanistha Buddhafield, there is much abundance and enjoyment. They live in palaces of variegated jewels and are also adorned with many gems and silks. That is an example of the great abundance. When we practice and make offerings, it is like the space treasury without end. In short, *sambhoga,* enjoyment, means "substances and wealth." Also, great power is needed in order to do vast things. With great power, you magnetize vast wealth, attendants, and students, people who follow you. Also, on the political level, you need to have power.

Magnetize harmonious companions, people with whom you have a good connection, which is not easy. Even a spouse with whom you have been living for many years and have had many children can be difficult. Couples argue, complain, and separate. Stay together with harmonious companions until you reach enlightenment. Jamyang Khyentse Wangpo and Chokgyur Lingpa were together as father and son for thirteen different lifetimes. This started with King Trisong Deütson and his son Murub

Tsenpo. Padmasambhava and Yeshe Tsogyal are still together in infinite buddhafields. Don't magnetize just anyone, but someone who can accomplish things. To condense it all to the essence, there is nothing in samsara and nirvana that Padma Khandro cannot magnetize.

If you do not wish to magnetize during the activity practice, you can do so during the recitation: Visualize yourself as Padma Khandro, with the HRIH syllable in your heart center and the mantra coiled around the seed syllable. As you recite OM KURU KULLE HRIH SOHA, lights radiate out and make offerings to the victorious ones. Gather back the blessings and accomplishments within you. This is the intention of the radiating, and it is all right, according to the commentary by Jamgön Kongtrül.

If, however, you do want to magnetize, then follow the instructions in the text and practice that way.

The HRIH syllables situated on the sun discs in the heart centers of the goddesses radiate red rays of light in the form of hooks. By merely touching the heart centers of whomever they wish to magnetize, those beings are brought under their power—just as a magnet gathers together all iron filings—and dissolve into the HRIH in the heart centers of the goddesses.

Do this visualization repeatedly, and during the recitation, sometimes remain without focus. Once again, do the visualization, and then again remain without focus; this is how you should train. If you practice in this way, by the power of deity, mantra, and samadhi, you will surely bring things under your control, just as ice placed in the hot sun cannot remain frozen. This is the intention of the outer practice.

PRACTICAL ADVICE

Concerning samadhi, you need to meditate, and Westerners really like to meditate. For meditation, nothing surpasses Dzogchen and maintaining rigpa. If you really know the meditation of Dzogchen and can sustain rigpa, you don't need to practice a deity. But if you are merely counting discursive thoughts, that has no benefit.

You need to do the mudras. Some people are doing them but most people sit with their hands inactive, which is the same as having no hands. You cannot really say that you cannot do them; you simply need to imitate someone doing them. There is nothing embarrassing about this. On the other hand, not knowing how to do them after practicing sadhana is embarrassing. So you must do the mudras. Doing just one mudra, like the opening lotus one, is more precious than doing one hundred thousand prostrations when taking refuge in the Mahayana vehicle. The movements of mudra in Vajrayana are great bliss. If you cannot do it well, you can improve. The benefits of mudra require so much explanation, in terms of the arranged channels, the moving pranas, and the essences, or tigles. The whole eighteenth chapter in the *Guhyagarbha Tantra* is devoted to explaining everything about mudra.

A *ngakpa* is a male yogi and a (*ngakma*) a female yogini, which you are. A yogi is someone who, having received empowerment, is practicing the three yogas. Dilgo Khyentse Rinpoche would sign his name as the yogi, doctrine holder, mangala, with no fixation at all in his mind; and *mangala,* good fortune, is Sanskrit for his Tibetan name Tashi Paljor. A yogi needs to know that he or she is a yogi. The yogi needs the view, meditation, and conduct. You need to perform a sadhana at least once a day.

There are many samayas for having received an empowerment. The most important samayas are the five buddha family samayas. For the jewel family, the samaya is to have a vajra and a bell and use them. All dharma practice is unifying skillful means and wisdom, illustrated by vajra and bell. It is said that you need to hold the vajra and bell perfectly.

You also need a good mala with the right characteristics. If you do not have a vajra and bell and a good mala, this indicates you are not a good practitioner. For food, you need to eat *mendrub*, lama medicine, everyday. To be a good practitioner of the Vajrayana, you need to first gather all the different necessary substances for practice, getting the objects with the right characteristics. This is easier than meditation. What I have spoken is the wisdom intent of the tantras.

Fruition

Yesterday, we finished the drubchen of magnetizing activity. Today, how are you? Have you really investigated that? It is good if you do so. There are many things to gather under your control, to magnetize, to bring into your power. Here, I am talking about bringing your mind under control. Yesterday, you finished receiving the accomplishments. This morning, if you, the practitioners, have had your mind pointed out according to Dzogchen, and have recognized the nature of mind—if while remaining in rigpa, your rigpa was more stable, clearer, and sharper, then you definitely accomplished the magnetizing activity. This only occurs through your own individual experience. When you examine, you know. It is not something learned. That is why it is very important to investigate this. If you are someone who does not practice this or does not rest in rigpa, then I have nothing to say to you.

If your mind truly became more clear and stable, then the prana becomes calmer. Then, naturally, mind's thoughts will be self-liberated. That is what "bringing under control" means. First, inwardly, you gain control over your mind; then, outwardly, all phenomena is brought under control. Once you completely control your own mind, male and female friends, lamas, and sponsors will be brought under control or magnetized. Thereafter, delusion no longer has any power over you. But if that is not the case, then you will fall under the power of deluded perceptions.

This is why I wanted you to examine what happened this morning. I thought that I needed to talk about it. All supreme and common accomplishments can be obtained. If you attain the supreme accomplishments, you automatically attain the common ones.

The water inside the vase is normally saffron water, but everyone was given alcohol. Also, inside the skull cup, there was beer. Once you drink this, the taste permeates your channels, and this happens in order to bring the mind's thoughts under control. If a practitioner gets a little drunk from alcohol, then rigpa becomes stronger, and coarse thoughts reduce, their strength diminishes. The small thoughts disappear. Due to the strength of alcohol, when you are a little drunk, the prana goes into the central channel. Since you received the siddhis yesterday, I wanted to talk about this. So, I would like you to examine from waking today, and see if you could rest in rigpa. If this happened very well, then you have attained magnetizing power. And once you have controlled your own mind, slowly you will be able to bring outer things into your power.

A PRAYER TO KURUKULLE[26]

Dzigar Kongtrul Rinpoche

དུས་གསུམ་རྒྱལ་བ་ཀུན་ཡུམ་ཕར་ཕྱིན་མ།

Düsum gyalwa kün-yum parchin ma

Prajñāpāramitā, mother of the three times victors,

ཐུགས་རྗེས་འགྲོ་བ་བསྒྲལ་མཛད་འཕགས་མ་སྒྲོལ།

Tukjé drowa dröldzé pakma dröl

Ārya Tārā, liberator of all beings through compassion,

ཁམས་གསུམ་ཆགས་པའི་དབང་མཛད་ཀུ་ར་ཀུལ་ལེ།

Khamsum chakpé wangdzé kurukullé

Kurukulle, magnetizer of the three realms through passion,

ཞལ་གཅིག་ཕྱག་བཞི་དམར་གསལ་པད་རག་མདོག

Zhalchik chakzhi marsal pérak dok

With one face and four arms, the clear color of ruby red,

འཛུམ་པའི་མདངས་ཀྱིས་བདག་ཡིད་སེམས་དཔར་བསྐྱེད།

Dzumpé dangkyi dak-yi sémpar kyé

Through your smiling expression, my mind gains the confidence of a sattva [bodhisattva-hero],

བསྟན་དང་འགྲོ་བའི་ལེགས་ཚོགས་བསྒྲུབ་པའི་ཕྱིར།

Tentang drowé léktsok drubpé chir

To excellently accomplish the purpose of the doctrine and beings.

---

26 Translated by Lama Chönam & Sangye Khandro

ཡན་ལག་བརྒྱད་ཀྱི་མཆོད་ཡོན་ཞབས་བསིལ་དང་།

Yenlak gyé-kyi chöyön zhabsil tang

Water of the eight qualities for drinking and bathing,

སྣ་ཚོགས་ལྡ་ན་སྡུག་པའི་མེ་ཏོག་དྲི།

Natsok tana dukpé metok dri

Fragrant varieties of lovely flora,

རབ་གསལ་མཁའ་མཉམ་ཉི་ཟླ་མར་མེའི་འོད།

Rabsal kha-nyam nyida marmé'i ö

The light of the extremely illuminating sun, moon, and butter lamps, equal to space,

ཡིད་འོང་བརྗིད་པར་བསྐྱེད་པའི་དྲི་ཆབ་དང་།

Yiong jipar kyépé drichab tang

Scented water that generates pleasure and majesty,

རོ་བརྒྱའི་ཞལ་ཟས་རོལ་མོ་དབྱངས་སྙན་བཅས། །

Ro-gyé zhalzé rolmo yang-nyen ché

Celestial delicacies of one hundred flavors, and the pleasing sounds of musical instruments,

ཕྱི་ནང་གསང་བའི་མཆོད་ཚོགས་ཀུན་བཟང་འཕྲུལ།

Chinang sangwé chötsok kunzang trül

A gathering of outer, inner, and secret offerings, like the emanations of Samantabhadra,

མ་ལུས་ནམ་མཁའ་རབ་འབྱམས་ཁམས་བཀང་ནས། །

Malü namkha rabjam khamkang né

To fill the regions of space without exception

འཕགས་མ་ཡིད་འོང་དཔལ་འབར་ཚོགས་ལ་འབུལ།

Pakma yiong palbar tsokla bül

Are offered to the glorious, blazing assembly of the lovely
Ārya Tārā,.

ཚོགས་གཉིས་རབ་རྫོགས་སྒྲིབ་གཉིས་ཡོངས་དག་ཅིང་།

Tsoknyi rabdzog dribnyi yongdak ching

May the two accumulations be perfected and the two obscurations
fully purified.

བར་ཆད་བདུད་ཀྱི་གཡུལ་ལས་རྒྱལ་བ་དང་།

Barché dü-kyi yullé gyalwa tang

May there be victory over the hordes of obstacle-creating māras.

ཕྱག་མཚན་ལྕགས་ཀྱུ་ཞགས་པའི་འོད་ཟགས་ཀྱིས། །

Chaktsen chak-kyu zhakpé özhak kyi

With your hand emblems, the iron hook and lasso of light,

འགྲོ་བ་ཀུན་རྣམས་བདག་གིས་དབང་གྱུར་ནས།

Drowa kün-nam dakgi wang-gyür né

May I magnetize all sentient beings,

ཐབས་ཀྱི་གཞུ་ལ་ཤེས་རབ་མདའ་དྲངས་ཏེ།

Tabkyi zhula shérab dadrang té

And with the bow of upāya and the arrow of prajñā drawn,

འཕགས་ལམ་ཡན་ལག་བརྒྱད་ཀྱི་དཔུང་དང་བཅས།

Paklam yenlak gyé-kyi pungtang ché

Along with the forces of the eight-branch path of the Āryas,

ངེས་ལེགས་ཐར་པའི་གནས་ལ་འགོད་པ་དང་།

Ngélek tarpé néla göpa tang

May I place all beings on the ground of definitive liberation.

གནས་སྐབས་སུ་འང་ཆོས་ནོར་ཚེ་གཡང་དང་།

Nekab suang chönor tséyang tang

For the time being, may everyone enjoy the Dharma, prosperity,

དཔལ་དང་འབྱོར་བ་ལོངས་སྤྱོད་རྒྱས་པ་དང་།

Paltang jorwa longchö gyépa tang

And longevity, and may glory and abundance be ever-increasing.

མ་ལུས་བསྟན་དང་འགྲོ་བའི་དོན་འགྲུབ་ཤོག

Malü tentang drowé döndrub shok

May the purpose of the doctrine and living beings be accomplished without exception!

ཅེས་པའང་ཀོང་སྤྲུལ་འཇིགས་མེད་པས་དགོས་ཆེད་འགས་བསྐུལ་ངོར་བྲིས་པས་འཕགས་མ་བྱིན་རླབས་དོན་ལྡན་འགྱུར་བར་ཤོག་ཅིག།

Thus, with a particular aim in mind, I, Kongtrul Jigme, (Dzigar Kongtrul Rinpoche), wrote this down with the prayer that the blessings of Ārya Tārā will reach meaningful fruition.

KURUKULLE FEAST[27]

Jamyang Khyentse Wangpo

༄༅། །རིགས་བྱེད་དབང་མོའི་ཚོགས་མཆོད་མདོར་བསྡུས་ནི།

Short Tsok Offering of the Powerful Lady Kurukulle

རཾ་ཡཾ་ཁཾ། ཚོགས་རྫས་ཤ་ལྔ་བདུད་རྩི་ལྔ།

Ram yam kham

Ram yam kham

Tsokdzé sha nga dütsi nga

The tsok substances of the five meats and five nectars,

ཡེ་ཤེས་རྣམ་ལྔ་ཞུ་བའི་བཅུད།

Yeshe nam nga shyuwé chü

The elixirs derived from the melting of the five wisdoms,

ཁ་དོག་དྲི་རོ་ནུས་པའི་གཏེར།

Khadok dri ro nüpé ter

Are a treasury of perfect color, smell, taste, and potency

འདོད་ཡོན་སྤྲིན་ཕུང་འཕྲོ་བར་གྱུར།

Doyen trinpung trowar gyur

Sending out vast clouds of sensory delights.

ཨོཾ་ཨཿཧཱུྃ་ཧ་ཧོ་ཧྲཱིཿ

Om ah hung ha ho hrih

Om ah hung ha hoh hrih

---

27 Translated by Han Kop

ཧྲཱིཿ རིགས་བདག་བླ་མ་འོད་དཔག་མེད།

Hrih, rikdak lama öpakmé

Hᴚɪʜ, Guru Amitābha, lord of the family,

ཡི་དམ་དབང་ཆེན་རྟ་མཆོག་དཔལ།

Yidam wangchen tachok pal

Glorious and powerful yidam deity Hayagrāva,

ཁྱད་པར་མཁའ་འགྲོ་རྒྱ་མཚོའི་གཙོ།

Khyepar khandro gyatsö tso

And, in particular, the consort Kurukulle, chief of infinite
dākinīs—

དྲན་པས་འཁོར་འདས་ཕུན་ཚོགས་ཀུན།

Drenpé khordé püntsok kün

By thinking of you, we bring all the abundance

དབང་མཛད་ཀུ་རུ་ཀུལླེ་ཡུམ།

Wang dzé kurukullé yum

Of samsāra and nirvana under our power.

འབུམ་ཕྲག་ཡངས་པའི་ཌཱ་ཀཱི་དང་།

Bumtrak yangpé daki dang

Hundreds of thousands of dākinīs,

ལྷ་ཆེན་མ་ཧཱ་དེ་བྭ་ཡབ།

Lhachen mahadeva yab

The consort—the great god Mahādeva—

བཙུན་མོ་ཨུ་མ་དེ་བྱི་སོགས།

Tsünmo umadewi sok

Goddess Umadevi, and all others

རབ་འབྱམས་དབང་གི་བཀའ་འཁོར་ཀུན།

Rabjam wang gi kakhor kün

In the infinite magnetizing retinue,

འདིར་གཤེགས་ཚོགས་ཀྱི་མཆོད་པ་བཞེས།

Dir shek tsok kyi chöpa shyé

Come here and enjoy this tsok offering!

སྲིད་ཞིའི་འདོད་ཡོན་རྒྱ་མཚོའི་སྤྲིན།

Sishyi döyön gyatsö trin

With infinite clouds of sensory delights of saṃsāra and nirvāṇa,

ནམ་མཁའ་མཛོད་ཀྱིས་ཐུགས་དམ་བསྐང་།

Namkha dzö kyi tukdam kang

A treasury as vast as the sky, may your wishes be fulfilled!

དམ་ཚིག་ཉམས་ཆག་ཉེས་ལྟུང་བཤགས།

Damtsik nyamchak nyetung shak

I confess my impairments, breakages, mistakes, and samaya
  downfalls!

བརྟན་གཡོའི་རྒུད་པ་མ་ལུས་སོལ།

Tenyö güpa malü sol

Dispel all degenerations of the world and beings!

ལེགས་ཚོགས་ཡོན་ཏན་ཐམས་ཅད་དང་།

Lek tsok yönten tamché dang

Bring all that is of benefit, all happiness and all good qualities,

ཁྱད་པར་དམིགས་ཡུལ་སྙིང་རྩ་སྒུལ།

Khyepar mikyul nying tsa gul

Without impediment, under our power.

ཐོགས་པ་མེད་པར་དབང་དུ་བསྡུས།

Tokpa mepar wang du dü

And, in particular, move the heart-channel of our object of focus,

བདག་ཅག་ཚེ་བསོད་དཔལ་འབྱོར་སྤེལ།

Dakchak tsesö paljor pel

Increase our life span, merit, and prosperity,

ལས་བཞི་གྲུབ་བརྒྱད་དབང་བཅུ་སོགས།

Lé shyi drub gyé wang chu sok

And make the four enlightened activities, the eight
accomplishments, the ten powers,

མཆོག་ཐུན་དངོས་གྲུབ་ཆར་ལྟར་ཕོབས།

Choktün ngödrub char tar pob

And the ordinary and supreme siddhis descend like rain!

ཨོཾ་གུ་རུ་དེ་བ་ཌཱ་ཀི་ནི་ཀུ་རུ་ཀུལླེ་ས་པ་རི་ཝཱ་ར་སརྦ་ག་ཎ་ཙཀྲ་པ་ཛ་ཧོ། མ་ཧཱ་བ་ལིཾ་ཏ་ཁ་ཧི།

Om guru déwa dakini kurukullé sapariwara sarva ganachakra
pudza ho | maha balingta khahi

OM GURU DEWA DAKINI KURU KULLE SAPARIVARA SARVA
GANACHAKRA PUDZA HOH

MAHA BALINGTA KHAHI

ཡིག་བརྒྱ་བརྗོད།

Recite the Hundred Syllable mantra.

*As a short feast prayer[28] to be repeated as many times as you wish, add the
following lines:*

Ram Yam Kham༔ Om Ah Hung༔
Om Ah Hung Om Kurur Kulle Hrih Svaha༔
Sapariwara Maha Ganachakra Puja Khakha Khahi Khahi༔
RAM YAM KHAM༔ OM AH HUNG༔
OM AH HUNG OM KURU KULLE HRIH SVAHA༔
SAPARIVARA MAHA GANACHAKRA PUDZA KHAKHA KHAHI
KHAHI ༔

Hung༔
Chomden khordang cheynam kyi Chopa gyamtso di shey shig༔

---

28 From the termas of Chokgyur Lingpa

DAKINI ACTIVITY

Nyamchag gyamtso malu shag Tugdam gyamtso malu kang༔
Ngodrub gyamtso tsal du sol Trinley gyamtso malu drub༔
Utsita Balingta Khakha Khahi Khahi༔

Hung༔
Blessed one, with your retinue,༔
Accept this ocean of offerings.༔
I confess an ocean of breaches.༔
May an ocean of wishes be fulfilled.༔
Bestow an ocean of siddhis.༔
Perfect an ocean of activities.༔
Utsita balingta khakha khahi khahi༔

REMAINDER

ཧྲཱིཿ དཀྱིལ་འཁོར་གཉེན་པོའི་མཐའ་སྐྱོང་བ༔

Hrih, kyilkhor nyenpö takyongwa

Hrīh! Hrih Guardians of the all-important mandala's boundary,

ལྷག་ལ་དབང་བ་དྲེགས་པའི་ཚོགས༔

Lhak la wangwa drekpé tsok

Hosts of arrogant ones who own the remainder,

འདིར་གཤེགས་བཟའ་བཏུང་ཚོགས་ལྷག་བཞེས༔

Dir shek zatung tsoklhak shyé

Come here and enjoy this tsok remainder of food and drink.

རྣལ་འབྱོར་བཅོལ་བའི་ཕྲིན་ལས་མཛོད༔

Naljor cholpé trinlé dzö

Carry out the activity entrusted by the yogis!

ཨུ་ཙི་ཏ་བ་ལི་ཏ་ཁ་ཧི༔

Utsita balingta khahi

Utsita balingta khahi

ASPIRATION

དབང་མཛད་མཁའ་འགྲོའི་ལྷ་ཚོགས་ལ།

Wangdzé khandrö lhatsok la
By making desirable offerings

འདོད་ཡོན་མཆོད་པ་ཕུལ་བ་ཡིས།

Döyön chöpa pulwa yi
To the gathering of magnetizing dākinīs,

རླུང་སེམས་སྣང་བ་དབང་དུ་འདུས།

Lungsem nangwa wang du dü
We bring wind-energy, mind, and perception under our power.

བདེ་ཆེན་ཡེ་ཤེས་འགྲུབ་པར་ཤོག

Dechen yeshe drubpar shok
May we accomplish the wisdom of great bliss!

ཅེས་སྨོན་ལམ་གདབ་བོ། མངྒ་ལཾ།

Mangalam!
MANGALAM!

ཞེས་པ་འདི་མཛད་བྱང་མི་གསལ་ཡང་། རྗེ་བླ་མ་འཇམ་དབྱངས་མཁྱེན་བརྩེའི་དབང་པོའི་
ཕྱག་བྲིས་འཁྲུལ་མེད་ལས་ཞལ་བཤུས་པ་ཡིན་པས་རྗེ་ཉིད་ཀྱི་གསུངས་ཡིན་པར་ངེས་
སོ་ཕྱིའི་དབང་པོའི་ཕྱག་བྲིས་འཁྲུལ་མེད་ལས་ཞལ་བཤུས་པ་ཡིན་པས་རྗེ་ཉིད་ཀྱི་གསུངས་ཡིན་པར་ངེས་
སོ། །

Although the colophon is illegible, since this was copied from the unmistakable handwriting of the lord guru Jamyang Khyentse Wangpo, it is certainly his own composition.

Fire Puja Mandala

VARIOUS WAYS
TO PRACTICE DAKINIS

THE INSTRUCTION OF
THE DAKINIS OF IMMORTALITY[29]

From Pema Tseyi Nyingtig

THE HEART ESSENCE OF LOTUS LIFE

A Terma Treasure of Jamyang Khyentse Wangpo

Homage to the wisdom dakini of immortality.

These essential instructions have three parts:
Development stage, completion stage, and empowerment.
First, for the meditation and recitation of the development stage,
Practice by means of preparation, the main part, and conclusion.
Samaya.

For the preparation, begin with refuge and bodhichitta, saying,

HRIH
I take refuge in the hosts of wisdom dakinis,
The realm of the unchanging bindu, the essence of existence and
    peace.
Generating bodhichitta for the welfare of all beings filling space,
I will accomplish the vidyadhara level of immortal life.

Second, expel obstructors and establish the protection boundary.
Purify the obstructor torma by saying,

RAM YAM KHAM

---

29 Translated by Erik Pema Kunsang

Consecrate it by chanting three times,

OM AH HUNG HA HOH HRIH

Summon the guests by saying,

SARVA BHUTA AKARKAYA JAH

Dedicate it three times by offering the sky treasury mantra and mudra,

SARVA BHUTE BHYO NAMAH SARVA TATHAGATA BAHYE BISHVA
MUKHE BHYE and so forth

HRIH
Life demons, obstacle-makers, and obstructors—ignorance
    occurring in progressive order—[30]
Disperse into the unconstructed expanse of awareness-wisdom!
Within the space of the Vajra Queen—the reverse order—
The unchanging and indestructible protection boundary is
    spontaneously accomplished.
HRIH VAJRA KRODHA HAYAGRIVA HULU HULU SARVA BIGHANAN
UCHITTA HUNG PHAT, VAJRA JNANA RAKSHA DHRUM

*Third, receive the downpour of blessings and consecrate the offerings by
saying,*

HRIH
The compassion of the deities of the Three Roots, flashing like
    lightning,
Showers down the splendor of wisdom display.
Consecrate the world and its contents as the pure outer, inner, and
    other[31]
To be the grand offering mudra!
OM AH HUNG, PADMA DAKINI CHANDALI JNANA ABESHAYA A
AH, HRIH SARVA PUJA MEGHA PANCHA AMRITA RAKTA BALINGTA
AH HUNG

For the samadhi of the main part, begin with the visualization of the samaya being:

HRIH꣬

Within the space of emptiness, the compassionate radiance of great
    bliss,꣬

A brilliant, red hrih appears like a rainbow.꣬

Its illuminating rays of light purify the solidity of the world and its
    beings.꣬

In this continuity of luminous emptiness, within the sphere of the
    five consorts,꣬

Amidst the crescent mansion of immortal life,꣬

In the center of the crossed source-of-dharma design endowed with
    the six wisdoms,꣬

Upon the lotus, sun, and moon of united means and knowledge,꣬

The syllable hrih transforms into Padma Chandali.꣬

The color of ruby, she smiles wrathfully with a passionate
    expression.꣬

Her three eyes are flashing, and her hair hangs free.꣬

Her breasts are full and the secret lotus has bloomed.꣬

Wearing a tiara of silken streamers, a shirt, and skirt,꣬

She is adorned with jewelry, bones, and flower garlands.꣬

The iron hook in her right hand captures the life essences of
    existence and peace,꣬

While the left proffers the excellent vase of longevity and wisdom.꣬

Her legs are in the dancing posture, with the left extended.꣬

She plays ravishingly within a scintillating sphere of light rays.꣬

Within her form is the complete mandala of the longevity deities of
    the Three Roots,꣬

And her head is crowned by Amitabha, the lord of the family.꣬

At the corners of the source-of-dharmas are the six vajra
    goddesses,꣬

The color of coral, their expressions are passionate and seductive.꣬

With the hooks in their right hands, they gather the pure essences

Of earth, water, fire, wind, space, and wisdom.꣬

The offering clouds of the six sense pleasures, billowing from their
    left hands,꣬

Generate the delight of great bliss in the chief lady of the family.§

Adorned with silks, jewels, and bone ornaments,§

They dance in dignified poses upon lotus flowers and moon discs.

Myriad deities and vidyadharas of longevity§

And millions of dakinis gather like cloud banks.§

The single gatekeeper is the red Lotus Lady of Space,§[32]

Who blazes in wrathful magnificence, holding the lotus knife and
skull.§

With the complete ferocious attire, she stands upon a lotus, sun,
and corpse,§

Her legs dancing in sporting poses amidst flames of wisdom.§

Gazing about, and uttering the sounds of hung! phat! pem!,§

She subdues the Lord of Death and the other four maras.§

The three places of the chief figure and the whole retinue are
marked with the three syllables.§

The hooks on the light rays invoke the hosts of wisdom beings§

To appear, filling the expanse of space; VAJRA SAMA JAH!§

Second, summon and dissolve the wisdom beings, saying,

HRIH§

Through your display of the spontaneously present expression of
awareness,§

Hosts of dakinis of immortality, arise from the space of primordial
purity and approach this place!§

Remain as the nondual samaya and wisdom beings!§

Without departing, bestow your blessings, life empowerment, and
siddhis!§

JNANA DAKINI MAHASUKHA E A RALLI HRING HRING PEM PEM§

JAH HUNG BAM HOH, SAMAYA TISHTHA LHAN§

Third, pay homage and make offerings, saying,

HRIH§

Like the gods who delight in magical display, I pay symbolic
homage.§

May you be pleased by this manifestation of Samantabhadra,§

A grand offering mudra of the five general sense pleasures, ⁞
Nectar, torma, rakta, union, deliverance, and great bliss! ⁞
HRIH JNANA DAKINI SAPARIVARA ARGHAM PADYAM PUSHPE
DHUPE ALOKE GANDHE NAIVIDYA SHABDA PRATICCHAYE SVAHA ⁞
SHAPTA SARVA PUJA HOH, MAHA PANCHA AMRITA RAKTA
BALINGTA KHAHI ⁞

Fourth, offer praise, saying,

HRIH ⁞
Dharmakaya Amitabha, sambhogakaya Amitayus, ⁞
Magical display Immortal Chandali, ⁞
Assembly of mandala deities of the Three Roots of longevity, ⁞
I praise you respectfully. Bestow the siddhi of immortality! ⁞

Fifth, generate the recitation intent, saying,

In the core of my heart, in the center of a lotus and moon, ⁞
Amidst the heart of Lord Amitayus with consort, ⁞
Is the sphere of the sun and moon marked with hrih and encircled
by the mantra. ⁞
The hooks on the light rays gather the life essences of samsara and
nirvana ⁞
In the form of nectar, which dissolves into hrih. ⁞
I thereby attain the supreme immortal life and wisdom. ⁞
OM AH HUNG PADMA CHANDALI AYUR JNANA SARVA SIDDHI HUNG ⁞

By reciting this four hundred thousand times, you will achieve immortality.

*Sixth, invoke the heart samaya by waving the life arrow and generating
deep yearning, as you say,*

HRIH ⁞
From the mandala of dharmadhatu, the purity of personal
experience, ⁞
Wisdom dakini Padma Chandali, ⁞
And your six vajra goddesses, taming whoever needs constraint, ⁞
Chief figure, with your retinue of emanations, manifest from
space! ⁞

Gather our vitality and life force, which have been cut, damaged, or dwindled away!

Collect the essences of earth, water, fire, wind, and space!

Amass the vitality, merit, and wisdom of samsara and nirvana!

Extend the interrupted life force and life span, by the truth of the nature of things!

Replenish degenerated health with nectar essences!

Bring back dwindled life energy with your lotus hooks!

Dissolve the pure essences of the animate and inanimate into the sadhana articles!

Confer the supreme empowerment of immortality upon the three doors of this yogi!

Bestow right now the siddhis of longevity and wisdom!

Recite the root mantra and then say,

TSHE DHRUM HRIH DZAH, GAYU DHRUM NRI DZAH, AYUR
JNANA GAYU TSHE dhrum nri dzah sarva siddhi phala hung

Repeat this again and again, sealing the dra-sign of longevity as the natural state of immortality.

HRIH

All the life essences of samsara and nirvana

Dissolve into the indestructible bindu and hrih.

In the inexpressible expanse of primordial purity,

They are again sealed beyond birth and death.

HRIH DHRUM AYUR JNANA A AH

For the concluding section, begin with the feast offering, saying,

RAM YAM KHAM

Within the vast lotus skull cup,

The feast articles of the five meats and five nectars,

The essence of the five families and five wisdoms,

Form a cloud bank of sense pleasures filling the sky.

OM AH HUNG HRIH

From the dharmadhatu palace of the three kayas,ཿ
Boundless Life Amitabha andཿ
Supreme consort, Goddess Chandali,ཿ
With your ocean-like retinue of the Three Roots,ཿ
Approach this place and accept these feast offerings!ཿ
I confess breaches of samaya, faults, and downfalls!ཿ
Liberate demons and obstacles to longevity into dharmadhatu!ཿ
Bestow the siddhis of longevity and wisdom!ཿ
HRIH PADMA JNANA CHANDALI SAPARIVARA GANA CHAKRA PUJA
HOHཿ

Repeat the Hundred Syllable mantra. At this point, you may perform any suitable version of the general or specific fulfillment-confession of the Three Roots. Then enjoy the feast accompanied by the symbolic (gestures for) offering and accepting.

Second, assign the residual portion, saying,

PANCHA AMRITA HUNG HA HOH HRIHཿ
The samaya residual portion becomes an inexhaustible mass of
    sense pleasures filling the sky.ཿ

HRIHཿ
Assemblages of dakinis, gings, and lankas,ཿ
Obeying the command of Padmeshvara,ཿ
Accept this residual torma of sense pleasures,ཿ
Prolong the life span of this yogi, and dispel obstacles!ཿ
MAMA DAKINI BALINGTA KHAHIཿ

Third, elicit the covenant, sustain the Tenmas, and perform the vajra horse dance, saying,

HRIHཿ
All guardians who were given the oathཿ
By the ocean of vidyadharas of the three lineagesཿ
Please approach, take this adorned torma,ཿ
And fulfill the activities in accordance with your promise!ཿ

HRIHཿ
True meaning of the natural purity of the twelve intervals,ཿ

Assemblage of Tenma goddesses,༔
Accept this nectar of cleansing water༔
And increase life span, splendor, and wealth!༔
Mama sing droma balingta khahi༔

Hrih༔
Summon and dissolve enemies, obstructors, and samaya violators༔
Into the depth of the flaming e, pit of the three realms!༔
On top, the Hayagriva Heruka༔
Seals it with the vajra dance.༔
E nri tri satvam bhaya nan༔

Fourth, receive the siddhis, make offerings, and praise, saying,

Hrih༔
Assemblage of immortal dakinis, approached and accomplished༔
Within the mighty crescent mandala of longevity,༔
Pay heed to me here with your loving compassion༔
And grant me the siddhis of body, speech, and mind!༔
Kaya vaka chitta siddhi phala hung༔

Amend duplications and omissions, and confess faults with the Vowels and Consonants and the Hundred-Syllable mantras.

Fifth, dissolve the development stage by saying,

Hrih༔
I and all appearances dissolve into the space of luminosity,༔
The original continuity of great emptiness.༔
Once more, like a wave rising from the waters,༔
I re-emerge in the magical form of visible emptiness.༔
Vajra raksha hang༔

Sixth, dedicate and make prayers of aspiration and auspiciousness, saying,

Hrih༔
By the power of the virtue of accomplishing the dakini of
    immortality,༔
May the life span, merit, and wisdom of all beings increase!༔

And may the goodness of the light of the supreme and common
siddhis⁜
Completely fill the world!⁜

*Seal with additional verses of auspiciousness. In the breaks, exert yourself
in gathering the two accumulations. Through this, obstacles to your life will
subside. If you persevere for a long time, you will attain immortality. Samaya.*

*Second, for the completion stage of longevity, assume the bodily posture
in a secluded place. Expel the stale breath, male, female, and neuter. Summon the essence of earth by vajra recitation. Bind it firmly within* HRIH *in
the heart center. Take in the essence of wind through the vase practice. Kindle
the essence of fire, the short* A *of tummo. Melt the essence of water into the
nectar of the letter* HANG. *Gather the essence of space, in the state of blissful
emptiness, mingle space and awareness, and rest in equanimity. If you practice
this one-pointedly, while possessing the pith instructions of the guru, you will
attain the immortal form of the rainbow body. Samaya.*

*Third, for conferring the empowerment of longevity, place the victory vase
filled with nectar within the source-of-dharmas marked with Mahadeva in a
red crescent-shaped mandala with one gate. To the right and left, arrange the
wine and pills of longevity. In front and behind, place the longevity torma and
the rainbow crystal. Arrange the offerings, feast articles, and so forth in the
general way. Follow the structure of the sadhana text and achieve the powers.
All disciples rinse with water. Give the torma for the obstructors and draw the
boundary of protection. Present a mandala offering and bring the following to
mind, saying,*

Single supreme teacher of great joy,⁜
Immortal Guru Chandali,⁜
Be kind and pay heed to me!⁜
Bestow the empowerment of wisdom and longevity!⁜

*Having made this request, take the oath, by putting nectar water upon the
tongue, placing the vajra at the hearts, and saying,*

If you pursue the siddhi of immortality,⁜
Lay the basis with faith and compassion,⁜
Observe the samayas, the meaning of empowerment, as your own
life,⁜

And exert yourselves in the profound path!

PANCHA AMRITA UTKA THA THA

Then utter the inviolable oath, saying,

SAMAYA ADANTE NARAKAN

Next, in the presence of the longevity deities of the Three Roots, filling the sky, take refuge, generate the bodhisattva resolve, and confirm the vows in the general way. No longer beholding the (other) disciples, within the state of emptiness, visualize the chief lady of the mandala along with the body mandala:

The Lord of the Family is at the crown,
The (Lady of Vajra) Form is at the eyes,
The (Lady of Vajra) Sound at the ears, Smell at the nose,
Taste at the tongue, Touch at the secret place,
And the Lady of Vajra Mind is in the heart center.
The wisdom being Amitayus resides in the core of her heart,
And the Lotus Queen of Space in her four limbs.
The all-encompassing longevity deities of the Three Roots fill all
    centers within her body.

Visualizing this, dissolve and stabilize the wisdom (beings).
Having invoked the heart samaya, now take the vase
    empowerment, saying,

HRIH
Within this auspicious vase, spherical like the unconstructed
    dharmakaya,
The inner contents of rupakaya appear, the mandala of the
    dakinis.
They melt into light, empowering me with the nectar of
    immortality.
May I obtain the vase empowerment of supreme body!

Recite the root mantra and then say,

KAYA ABHIKENTSA OM

For the secret empowerment, take nectar from the skull, saying,

HRIH

By empowering me with the essence bodhichitta
Of Guru Immortal Wisdom, Chandali
In union with Lotus Amitayus,
May I obtain the secret empowerment of supreme speech!
VAKA ABHIKENTSA AH

For the knowledge empowerment, take the pill of nectar-extract, saying,

HRIH

By taking this longevity pill of nectar-extract,
The essences of existence and peace in the form of the unchanging
    sphere,
May the power and strength of the nadis, pranas, bindus, and four
    joys blaze forth,
And may I obtain the great bliss empowerment of supreme mind!
CHITTA ABHIKENTSA HUNG

For the fourth, indicate with the symbol of the rainbow crystal, saying,

HRIH

The essence of mind itself is primordially pure like a crystal.
The play of spontaneous presence manifests like rainbow colors.
By empowering me with their indivisible innate nature,
May I obtain the awareness-expression empowerment of supreme
    wisdom!
JNANA ABHIKENTSA A AH

*As the concluding support, place the torma of longevity at the crown of
your head:*

HRIH

Conqueror Amitabha, lord of dharmakaya,
Amitayus, protector of the fivefold sambhogakaya,
Chandali, immortal nirmanakaya,
Padmasambhava, the indivisibility of the three kayas,
Mandarava, lady of space and owner of longevity,

King, subject and companion Nubchen Namkhai Nyingpo, and
others,[333]
Assemblage of knowledge-holders and dakinis, who have
accomplished immortality,
I invoke your samaya; bring forth the majestic splendor of
compassion!

For us noble children, the worthy disciples,
Bring back the vitality and life force, which have been cut,
damaged, or dwindled away!
Dispel into the space of luminosity the obstacles to longevity!
Dissolve the pure essences of samsara and nirvana into the bindu
within our hearts!
Bestow the supreme and common siddhis of longevity and
wisdom
Within the expanse of the youthful vase body beyond birth and
death!
SARVA SIDDHI ABHIKENTSA HRIH

*Next, seal the essence of longevity, give the articles of auspiciousness, and
perform the enthronement. All (the disciples) take the samaya pledge and offer
the thanksgiving. Turn the "gathering wheel" (ganachakra) of a feast banquet.
Thus, by conferring this eminent and profound empowerment, all become
suitable vessels for the path. It pacifies the fear of untimely death and increases
life span, merit, and wisdom. Since all disciples will ultimately accomplish the
body of immortality, all destined people should treasure this dearly. Samaya.*

*This is the extracted essence of one billion tantras of vajra life, the very
heart of the self-appeared Padma. I give this as an ultimate secret path for the
present assembly of the king and subjects and for the practice of the vidyadharas, who will tame beings in the future, in the form of a dharani of five-colored
letters within a casket of the sphere of space and awareness.*

*It is entrusted to the dakinis, and when at some point the time of the aus-
picious coincidence arrives, as indicated by the profound mind transmission,
may the nectar of instruction of the hearing lineage cause the destined ones to
accomplish immortality!*

Samaya. Seal. Seal. Seal. Guhya. Sign dissolved

Through the blessings of the great Master of Uddiyana, the knower of the three times, this was established (in writing) by Padma Do-ngak Lingpa Ösel Trülpey Dorje.[34]

This (edition) of the uncorrupted treasure root text, joined together with minor additional remarks, was written down by Lodrö Thaye, in accordance with the command of the Guru.[35]

Vajra Daka Dakini

FOUR ACTIVITIES[36]

Padmasambhava and Chokgyur Lingpa

When, through Approach, you have invoked the heart samayas,
And, through Accomplishment, you have been endowed with the
    capacity
To attain whichever siddhis you may desire,
You should achieve them through the stages of the four activity
    applications.

When practicing the pacifying activity,
Face east at dawn.
In the sattva posture, recite the chanting tune
Gently, quietly, and in a relaxed manner.
For the visualization of the emanation-absorption of the samadhi,
Sustain a peaceful, clear frame of mind and imagine as follows:

Dak dün kyilkhor lhatsok lé
From me and all the mandala deities in front,

Özer dütsi rangshyin trö
Nectar-like light rays stream forth,

Dorje khandrö tukgyü kul
Invoking the minds of the Vajra Daka and Dakini.

dé lé özer karpo trö
The white rays of light radiating from them

Tongsum jikten kham künkhyab
Permeate the entire billionfold world system.

Nedön dikdrib jepur dang
Sickness, evil forces, misdeeds, veils, curses,

---

36 Translated by Erik Pema Kunsang

Jikpa gyé dang chudruk sok⁞

The eight and sixteen fears, and⁞

Mitün chok kün rabtu shyi⁞

All discordant factors are completely pacified.⁞

Tsur dü dak la timpa yi⁞

As they gather back and dissolve into me,⁞

Shyiwé lé kün drubpar gyur⁞

All the pacifying activities are accomplished.⁞

Attach this at the end of the root mantra:⁞

HA BENZA DAKINI RA BENZA GINGKARA OM SHANTIM KURU SOHA⁞

At times, emanate and absorb bodily forms⁞
As well as mantra garlands and attributes.⁞
Thus, by exerting yourself in the specifics for single sessions,⁞
Within a certain number of weeks and days,⁞
In actuality, disharmony will be pacified,⁞
And you will achieve the true speech that benefits others.⁞
In dreams, you will bathe and wear new clothes,⁞
And you will go beyond fearful places, and so forth.⁞
These are taught to be the signs of having accomplished the pacifying
*   activity.*⁞
Samaya.⁞

When practicing the activity of increasing favorable conditions,⁞
Face south at sunrise.⁞
In the reveling posture, recite the chanting tune⁞
Melodiously, slowly, and in a dignified manner.⁞
For the visualization of the emanation-absorption of the samadhi,⁞
Sustain a magnificent, awe-inspiring frame of mind and imagine as
*   follows:*⁞

Dak dün kyilkhor lhatsok lé⁞

From me and all the mandala deities in front⁞

Nyima charké ö tar trö⁞

Light rays stream forth, like a rising sun,⁞

Ratna Daka Dakini

Rinchen khandrö tukgyü kul
Invoking the minds of the ratna daka and dakini.

Dé lé özer serpo trö
The yellow rays of light radiating from them

Tongsum jikten kham künkhyab
Permeate the entire billionfold world system.

Tsé dang sönam paljor dang
Life span, merit, splendor, wealth,

Tob dang nyendrak yeshe sok
Strength, fame, wisdom, goodness, and

Tünkyen lek tsok rabtu gyé
All favorable conditions are fully increased.

Tsur dü dak la timpa yi
As they gather back and dissolve into me,

Gyepé lé kün drubpar gyur
All the increasing activities are accomplished.

RI RATNA DAKINI TSA RATNA GINGKARA DHRUM PUSHTIM
KURU OM

In actuality, favorable conditions will increase
And you will effortlessly gather food, wealth, and enjoyments.
In dreams, plants and trees will spring up and rivers will swell,
Many people will gather, and so forth.
These are taught to be the signs of having accomplished the increasing
* activity.*
Samaya.

When practicing the activity of magnetizing desirable things,
Face west in the evening.
In the lotus posture, recite the chanting tune
In a manner that is passionate and attached.
For the visualization of the emanation-absorption of the samadhi,
Sustain a yearning, wishful frame of mind and imagine as follows:

Padma Daka Dakini

Dak dün kyilkhor lhatsok lé༔
From me and all the mandala deities in front,༔

Özer jé chak rangshyin trö༔
Rays of light, the nature of passion, stream forth,༔

Pema khandrö tukgyü kul༔
Invoking the minds of the Padma Daka and Dakini.༔

Dé lé özer marpo trö༔
The red rays of light radiating from them༔

Tongsum jikten kham künkhyab༔
Permeate the entire billionfold world system.༔

Lhami nöjin tobden dang༔
Powerful gods, humans, yakshas,༔

Zé nor longchö ngatang sok༔
Food, wealth, enjoyments, dominion, and༔

Yitün tamché wang du dü༔
All desirable things are brought under control.༔

Tsur dü dak la timpa yi༔
As they gather back and dissolve into me,༔

Wang gi lé kün drubpar gyur༔
All the magnetizing activities are accomplished.༔

NI PEMA DAKINI HRIH PEMA GINGKARA HRIH WASHAM KURU
HOH༔

In actuality, food, wealth, and women will be gathered,༔
And you will be able to change the perception of others effortlessly.༔
In dreams, you will ride on the sun and moon,༔
Drink up an ocean, traverse the four continents, and so forth.༔
These are taught to be the signs of having accomplished the magnetizing
activity.༔
Samaya.༔

When practicing the wrathful activity of annihilating,༔
Face north at dusk.༔
Then, in the fierce posture, recite the chanting tune༔

Karma Daka Dakini

In the manner of a great, pummeling hailstorm. ᦷ
For the visualization of the emanation-absorption of the samadhi, ᦷ
Sustain a ferocious, violent frame of mind and imagine as follows: ᦷ

Dak dün kyilkhor lhatsok lé ᦷ
From me and all the mandala deities in front, ᦷ
Özer tsa shying tsubpa trö ᦷ
violent, sparking rays of light stream forth, ᦷ

Lé kyi khandrö tuk gyü kul ᦷ
Invoking the minds of the karma daka and dakini. ᦷ

Dé lé özer tingnak trö ᦷ
The dark blue rays of light radiating from them ᦷ

Tongsum jikten kham künkhyab ᦷ
Permeate the entire billionfold world system. ᦷ

Dralwé shying chu nyampa dün ᦷ
The ten objects to be liberated, the seven transgressors, ᦷ

Damsi jungpo dön gek sok ᦷ
The samaya violators, elemental forces, evil spirits, obstructors, and ᦷ

Marung tamché tsarché ching ᦷ
All vicious spirits are annihilated. ᦷ

Lar dü dak la timpa yi ᦷ
As they gather back and dissolve into me, ᦷ

Drakpö lé kün drubpar sam ᦷ
All the wrathful activities are accomplished. ᦷ

SA KARMA DAKINI YA KARMA GINGKARA HUNG MARAYA PHAT ᦷ

In actuality, the enemies of the doctrine will pass away, ᦷ
And omens will appear, indicating that the haughty spirits have been subdued. ᦷ
In dreams, lakes will dry up, rocks will crumble, ᦷ
You will kill vicious animals, and so forth. ᦷ
These are taught to be the signs of having accomplished the wrathful activity. ᦷ

Samaya.

Then, for the supreme activity application,
The practice of the group gathering,
Practice correctly,
According to the elaborate sadhana section of the Kadü.
Having completed the four aspects of Approach and Accomplishment,
At dusk, invoke the minds of the deities.
At midnight, receive the siddhi of liberating.
At dawn, take union onto the path.
By means of such yogas,
You will attain the four vidyadhara levels in this lifetime.

E MA, *this wonderful and amazing path*
Is the journey taken by the jinas of the three times.
Samaya. Seal. Seal.

For the specific, individual practices
Of the twelve power-wielding vidyadharas,
Place each, in turn, in the position of the chief figure,
And place the chief figure in his position.
Follow the order of the activities to any suitable extent,
And condense Approach and Accomplishment into one.
By maintaining the yogas, practice this path
For quickly achieving whichever siddhi you desire.
Samaya. Seal. Seal.

Of the entire Lamey Tukdrub,
The inner practice is like my heart.
Within it, like the essence of my heart blood,
I, Padma, have now completely taught
This most profound intent of visualization
To the king, father, and son.
Lovingly considering the future suffering
Of the destitute Tibetan people,
Tsogyal committed this to writing
And concealed it as a precious essence of earth.
Signs will indicate when the time for its disciples has come:
Everywhere throughout India, Nepal, and Tibet,

Outer and inner fighting and strife will occur repeatedly.

There will be a sudden outbreak of plague for human beings and
    cattle.

The assemblies of the great beings upholding the doctrine

Will fall subject to sudden obstacles,

Or, with their minds influenced by demonic forces,

They will behave in all kinds of improper ways.

At that time, this profound instruction

Will benefit Tibet in general

And all central countries in particular.

It will then greatly extend the duration of the teachings of the Buddha.

Thus, he spoke.

I, Tsogyal, wrote down exactly what he had spoken and concealed it as a secret, supreme treasure. Samaya. Seal. Seal. Seal.

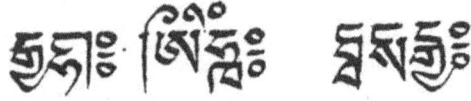

This is a genuine secret of the profound treasures of the emanation of Prince Damdzin, the undisputed and timely incarnated great treasure revealer Orgyen Dechen Lingpa.

Chokling Chö

THE OFFERING AND GIVING OF THE BODY[37]

According to Tukdrub Sheldam Nyingjang, the Heart Essence Practice Manual of Oral Instructions

Padmasambhava and Chokgyur Lingpa

First, take refuge and generate bodhichitta by reciting,

Namo
Dagsog drokün jangchub bar
Tsawa sumla kyabsu chi
Zhendön sangye tobjey chir
Lükyi chöjin gompar gyi

NAMO
From now until reaching enlightenment, I and all other beings
Take refuge in the Three Roots.
In order to attain enlightenment for the benefit of others,
I will train in the offering and giving of the body.

Then enact the actual giving of the body by saying,

Pey
Rangsem machö tröma nag
Tsangpey lamney gyang-gi tön
Ösel yingkyi namka la
Rigpa rangnang chag-gyar shar
Chag-ye dorjey drigug gi
Ranglü pungpo dumbur tub
Tongsum dangnyam töpey nang
Yeshe dütsi gyamtsor kyil
Langpa döyön ngaden pey

37 Translated by Erik Pema Kunsang

Chötrin khadang nyampar pel
Zagmey dewa chenpö dzey
Peldrib drelwey gyendu gyur
Om ah hung

PHAT
Unfabricated mind, the Black Wrathful One,
Emerges through the path of Brahma and shoots far off.
Within the sky of luminous space,
The mudra of self-manifest awareness appears.
With the vajra knife in her right hand,
She cuts asunder the aggregate of my body.
Within the skull cup, as vast as the billionfold universe,
Wisdom nectars flow together like an ocean.
Their vapors expand, becoming offering clouds
Of the five sense pleasures as vast as the sky.
This substance of unconditioned great bliss
Becomes an ornament beyond both increase and decrease.
OM AH HUNG

Pey
Nangsi nöchü tamchey kün
Döney namdröl chag-gya che
Ösel gyumey rölpa ley
Sizhi chir-yang nangwey drön
Choktsam teng-og küntu kyab
Dro-ong mepey gongpar del
Tamchey ronyam chenpö ngang
Könchok tsasum gyamtso chö

PHAT
All that appear and exist, the world and beings,
Are, primordially, the great mudra of liberation.
Out of the magical play of luminosity,
All possible experiences of existence and peace are the guests
Pervading all directions: cardinal, intermediate, above, and below,
Vastly unfolding the realization beyond coming and going.
In this state of the great equal taste of all things,
I make offerings to the Three Precious Ones and the Three Roots.

Chökyong sungmey tukdam kang
Gek-rik lenchag tsimchir jin
Rikdrug nyingje tsokla ngo
Zagmey dütsi chöjin gyi
Gyeshing nyeney rabtsim tey
Sönam tsokchen lhüngyi drub
Yeshe ösel tsölmey shar
Khorsum tsenma ledey pey
Dömey neluk ngöngyur shog
Pey

May the samaya with the dharma protectors and guardians be mended.
I give this so that all obstructors and karmic debtors may be satisfied.
I give this to the six classes of beings, who are the objects of compassion.
With this offering and giving of unconditioned nectar,
May you be utterly pleased and satisfied.
As the great accumulation of merit is spontaneously perfected,
Wisdom luminosity dawns effortlessly.
May the original state be realized,
Beyond the concept of the three spheres.
PHAT

Uttering this, rest in the state beyond focus.

Jinpa gyachen gyurpa diyi tü
Drowey döndu rangjung sangye shog
Ngöngyi gyalwa namkyi madrel wey
Kyewö tsoknam jinpey drölgyur chig

By the power of offering this immense gift,
May there be self-existing awakening for the benefit of all beings!
May all beings who were not liberated by the victorious ones of the past
Be liberated through this act of giving.

The preliminary and concluding liturgies were composed by Dilgo Khyentse, Mangalam.

This short, essential Chö practice is in Guru Rinpoche's own words, as revealed in the form of a terma by the great tertön Chokgyur Lingpa.

COMMENTARY ON THE OFFERING AND GIVING OF THE BODY[38]

According to Tukdrub Sheldam Nyingjang, the Heart Essence Practice Manual of Oral Instructions

Tulku Urgyen Rinpoche

This sadhana, called *Offering and Giving of the Body,* is taken from *Tukdrub Sheldam Nyingjang,* which is the root text of the *Tukdrub Barchey Künsel.* This is in Guru Rinpoche's own words. By practicing this sadhana, you will accumulate great merit.

Chö means the "cutting practice." In general, you practice by imagining that your mind, in the form of black Vajrayogini or some other form of Vajrayogini, shoots out through your head. Then you give this offering of your body to the four kinds of guests: The Three Jewels, meaning buddhas, bodhisattvas, and so forth; the protectors; all six classes of sentient beings; and then evil spirits and other negative influences.

After the nature of your mind, in the form of the black goddess, flies out of the top of your head, she then turns back, wielding a huge curved knife with a vajra handle in her right hand. All dakinis carry this type of knife when doing this kind of practice. In their left hand, they hold a skull cup filled with blood. The curved knife symbolizes cutting through birth and death. You do this by severing ignorance at its very root, as the twelve links of independent origination are cut at the very source, so there is no birth and death in samsaric existence. That is why she wields the knife. The blood symbolizes the habitual tendencies of ego-clinging, misdeeds, confused thinking, and so forth. These become the form of blood that is drunk without leaving any remnants whatsoever. Thus, the very source or root of samsara is utterly obliterated. That is why black Vajrayogini holds the knife in her hands.

---

38 Translated by Erik Pema Kunsang

Then, with a single chop, she cuts a piece of your skull off and turns it upside down. Then, all by themselves, three small skulls appear below it, supporting it like a stand. This tripod resembles three stones you place to support the cooking pot when you're camping, except these three appear by themselves. At the same time, imagine that you use the knife to cut your own normal physical body into small pieces; then throw everything into the skull cup. It gets cooked into a nice soup by the natural heat we have under the navel. When taking birth from the two essences of the father and mother, the white and red elements, we are endowed with natural heat and natural nectar. These are the red element below the navel and the white element at the crown of the head; both are always present.

Present here is the fire, which burns below and cooks everything within the nectar. At the same time, imagine that the whole thing expands, so your skull becomes as huge as a galaxy, containing the whole billionfold universe within it; everything is within your skull. When it is well cooked, vapors in the form of rainbow light stream forth, filling space in all directions. The light turns into all different kinds of sense objects, like beautiful sights and scenery, sweet sounds, pleasant fragrances, tastes, textures, and so forth—whatever is pleasing.

You then call upon the four types of guests again, which are the Three Jewels, including all masters, yidams, and dakinis; all the dharma protectors and guardians of the teachings; all sentient beings of the six realms, meaning all hell beings, hungry ghosts, animals, human beings, demigods, and gods; [and, finally, evil spirits and other negative influences]. They all gather around, with the enlightened ones above you and the unenlightened ones below you. Further below are all the negative forces, evil spirits who make obstacles for dharma practice, like your direct and indirect material enemies. All of them are invited as guests to partake in this huge feast. It is like throwing a big party of wisdom-nectar.

The traditional practice of Chö has a section for each of the four types of guests. These are sometimes called the white feast, the red feast, the multicolored feast, and the black feast, in which you offer different kinds of things. But since this is Guru Rinpoche's pith instruction condensed into one page, everything is offered together.

First, take refuge and generate bodhichitta by reciting,

NAMO

From now until reaching enlightenment, I and all other beings
Take refuge in the Three Roots.

I and all other beings refers to all sentient beings of the six realms. *Take refuge in the Three Roots* indicates the root of blessings, which is the guru; the root of accomplishment, which is the yidams; and the root of activities, which is the dakinis.

In order to attain enlightenment for the benefit of others,
I will train in the offering and giving of the body.

In order to attain enlightenment not only for yourself but also for all six classes of sentient beings without exception, you are pledging to gather the accumulations, both with and without focus—meaning both merit and wisdom. The practice contained here is supreme in both purifying all obscurations and also gathering the accumulations of merit and wisdom.

Then enact the actual giving of the body by saying,

PHAT⁞

By uttering PHAT, you start out from the very beginning with a thorough cut, Trekchö. You want to cut through ego-clinging, which is the source and root of all evil attachment to your body, to yourself, such as when you think, "I will get sick, I will suffer, I am too cold, I am too hot, I am hungry, I am thirsty," and so forth. To cut through that with the view, you first shout, PHAT.

At the beginning of Chö practice, there is a section called "identifying who is the mother of all buddhas," in other words recognizing the view. That is the reason for shouting PHAT at the outset. So, you begin with the samadhi of suchness. Then the first line reads,

Unfabricated mind, the Black Wrathful One,⁞
Emerges through the path of Brahma and shoots far off.⁞

The Black Wrathful One is black Vajrayogini, Tröma Nagmo, who is no other than your own unfabricated *mind.* Wandering in samsara occurs only when mind is fabricating concepts and being confused. But if mind is left all to itself, without any artifice or fabrication whatsoever, then the nature of mind is revealed as the dharmakaya. Black Vajrayogini is the dharmakaya of your own mind, which is revealed in that moment. Dharmakaya refers to your mind, not your physical body, which is called the "body of karmic ripening." In order to purify this fabrication and confusion, black Vajrayogini comes out of the top of your head and flies off into the distance, just like an arrow shot out of the body.

Within the sky of luminous space,⁓

Buddhahood has two aspects, space (bying) and awareness (rigpa). Space is the empty side and rigpa is the cognizant side. So, within the sky of luminous space.

The mudra of self-manifest awareness appears.⁓

Here, *mudra* means the bodily form of the goddess, which is personal experience (*rang nang*). Here we have both space and awareness together.

> With the vajra knife in her right hand,⁓
> She cuts asunder the aggregate of my body.⁓
> Within a skull cup, as vast as the billionfold universe,⁓
> Wisdom nectars flow together like an ocean.⁓
> Their vapors increase, becoming offering clouds⁓
> Of the five sense pleasures as vast as the sky.⁓
> This substance of unconditioned great bliss⁓
> Becomes an ornament beyond both increase and decrease.⁓
> OM AH HUNG⁓

After emerging from the head of your normal physical body, your nature of mind, which is indivisible space-awareness, takes the form of Vajrayogini called *rang nang chagya*, meaning the "natural form of your own experience." In her right hand, she has a curved knife with a vajra handle. Cutting your physical body into pieces, she throws it into a *skull cup as vast as the billionfold universe. Billionfold* means a thousand times a thousand times a thousand, thus, one billion universes all together. The skull cup is that large.

Its cooked contents become like an ocean of *wisdom nectars*. Here, *wisdom* implies that the contents are not material but empty forms. *Their vapors*, the steam that comes up, become the five sense pleasures in a huge cloud that spreads and covers the expanse of space with offerings. These are called the "articles of great bliss," which are unconditioned and undefiled. They are not material or normal kinds of articles, but undefiled and unconditioned (*zagmey dewa*) offerings that are an adornment of space. As all phenomena have actually been transformed into unceasing and changeless offerings, they neither increase nor decrease. Then you repeat OM AH HUNG many times. OM AH HUNG purifies, transforms, and increases the body, speech, and mind of all the buddhas. At this point, chant OM AH HUNG quite a few times. Then again return to the view, shout PHAT once, and then chant,

> All that appear and exist, the world and beings,
> Are, primordially, the great mudra of liberation.

From the very beginning, everything is Mahamudra, the great forms of the complete liberation.

> Out of the magical play of luminosity,
> All possible experiences of existence and peace are the guests
> Pervading all directions: cardinal, intermediate, above, and below,
> Vastly unfolding the realization beyond coming and going.
> In this state of the great equal taste of all things,
> I make offerings to the Three Precious Ones and the Three Roots.

Here the word *magical* is not like normal magic, which is created by dualistic mind; it is "wisdom magic" that is immaterial and unconditioned. Out of this wisdom magic, all phenomena that appear and exist, all of samsara and nirvana, are the guests as well. This offering cloud spreads in all directions: above and below, cardinal and intermediate.

This transcends the ordinary method of Chö practice, because it is combined with the view. Here, you don't hold any notions of impurity or recipients, because everything is "the continuity of deity, mantra, and wisdom." In this way, you combined it with the view, which is the great all-pervasive wisdom mind, which is neither coming nor going; everything is in the *state of the great equal taste*. Here, *equal taste* simply means being free from grasping, free from accepting and rejecting. In that state, whatever you experience is, by itself, the *great equal taste*. You offer this to *the Three Precious Ones and the Three Roots*. That is the first of the normal offerings. Then, by this:

> May the samaya with the dharma protectors and guardians be mended. ⁑

That is the second one.

> I give this so that all obstructors and karmic debtors may be satisfied. ⁑

This is the third one. Then comes the fourth one:

> I give this to the six classes of beings, who are the objects of compassion. ⁑

The four types of guests are as mentioned above.

> With this offering and giving of unconditioned nectar, ⁑
> May you be utterly pleased and satisfied. ⁑

Here, you refers to everybody.

> As the great accumulation of merit is spontaneously perfected, ⁑
> Wisdom luminosity dawns effortlessly. ⁑

This concludes the accumulations of both merit and wisdom. Then you finish off with good wishes.

> May the original state be realized ⁑
> Beyond the concept of the three spheres. ⁑

The aspiration here is that everyone may realize the primordial state, the original state, the buddha nature—which lies beyond any attributes of the three spheres. *The concept of the three spheres* refers to the act of giving, the object of the offerings, and the one who gave them. So, your offering should be totally beyond any of these concepts.

PHAT

Uttering this, rest in the state beyond focus.

That is the end of the practice, followed by four lines to dedicate the merit.

> By the power of offering this immense gift,
> May there be self-existing awakening for the benefit of all beings!
> May all beings who were not liberated by the victorious ones of the
>   past
> Be liberated through this act of giving.

The preliminary and concluding liturgies were composed by Dilgo Khyentse, Mangalam.

The first four lines and the last four were written by Dilgo Khyentse Rinpoche; the rest was written by Guru Rinpoche, himself.

Combining this with the view, you have a perfect way of condensing all Chö practice into a short sadhana that was written by Padmasambhava. Karmey Khenpo made a longer version that is thirteen pages, but this is the essence of all of it.

The following two lines are extremely significant:

> May the original state be realized,
> Beyond the concept of the three spheres.

The three spheres (khor sum) are the three things you usually hold in mind. Normally, when you give something, you are the one giving it and someone is receiving it. However, this gesture here transcends the attributes of the three spheres. Thus, you no longer hold anything in mind in regard to sentient beings and other objects of offering; the different kinds of feast distributions, which are the articles being given; and also you, yourself, who gives them. Totally transcending this, *may the original state be realized.*

The original state is the self-existing wakefulness, which is the true Samantabhadra. The form of Samantabhadra is, of course, just an image; this is the relative or symbolic form of Samantabhadra. But the ultimate Samantabhadra is self-existing wakefulness, which is the original state of the mind. So, may this be realized.

The four kinds of banquets are like parties, where you give something to everyone. At the white banquet, you give the three white things to certain types of beings. At the red banquet, you give blood to certain other types. The multicolored banquet contains whatever sentient beings desire—anything, like mansions, farmers' fields, or riches. Offering any possible thing that sentient beings desire is the multicolored banquet. Finally, at the black banquet, rotten pus, blood, and tar are actually offered to certain kinds of beings to whom you owe karmic debts. You imagine giving away all your negative karma, habitual tendencies, obscurations, and so forth, in the form of these disgusting things. Since you owe them a karmic debt, they are happy and satisfied with the black banquet and these offerings. By making them happy, you clear the debt, which transforms their unvirtuous frame of mind into a virtuous one. All of these are essentially included within this one text.

This sadhana combines the intent of both Sutra and Tantra traditions into a single practice. Actually, the very basis or root of Chö practice comes from the Prajñ p ramit sutra called the *Sutra Compendium of Transcendental Knowledge*. Within this sutra, the Buddha taught three types of samadhi called the "vajra-like samadhi," the "samadhi of the courageous journey," and the "magic-like samadhi." The first one, the vajra-like samadhi, corresponds to the samadhi of suchness, which is recognition of the nature of mind. The samadhi of the courageous journey is nothing other than great compassion, which manifests in emptiness when you recognize the nature of mind. The third, the magic-like samadhi, is often referred to as the "samadhi of the seed-syllable." Within this, you visualize that whatever beings desire arises out of this magic and is given to them. These compose the basic intent of Chö practice, as taught by the Buddha himself in that sutra.

Sangwa Yeshe

CLOUD BANK OF GREAT BLISS[39]

The supplication to the Lineage of the Dakini Sangwa Yeshe
from the Treasure Vase of Profound Instructions

Composed by Chokling Pema Gyurmey

Great dharmakaya mother, devoid of all constructs,
Queen of the five families, with the five certainties complete,
Sangwa Yeshe, manifest as the nirmanakaya,
I supplicate you. Grant the coemergent wisdom!

Lord of Secrets, Leykyi Wangmo,
Padmasambhava and longevity consort Mandarava,
Yeshe Tsogyal, Lhasey, and consort,
I supplicate you. Grant the coemergent wisdom!

Holders of the treasuries of transmission, Chokgyur Dechen
   Lingpa,
Khyentse Wangpo, and Lodrö Thaye;
Two sons of the noble family; and lineage masters,
I supplicate you. Grant the coemergent wisdom!

Within the outer and inner vajra mandala of the world and beings,
Dances the wisdom dakini, the great bliss of aware emptiness.
May this fully perfected actuality, in the form of Sangwa Yeshe,
Be realized within this very life and body!

This was written at Tsopema, in the Noble Land (India), as a necessary
implement by Chokling Pema Gyurmey.

---

39 Translated by Erik Pema Kunsang

THE FULFILLMENT OF ALL WISHES[40]

The Sadhana of Dakini Sangwa Yeshe from the Essence
Manual entitled Plentiful Vase of Profound Instructions[41]

Padmasambhava and Chokgyur Lingpa

*Bowing down to the creator of the wisdom of great bliss, who magne-
tizes experience and mind, I here condense the numerous instructions
to their essence for the resplendence of everyone wishing to practice.*

*This practice is the condensed version of the quintessence of a hundred
thousand dakinis' numerous instructions. It is comprised of three parts:
the preparation, main part, and conclusion.*

PREPARATION

*First, in an auspicious place, on a day such as the tenth day of the waxing
moon, arrange a dakini torma consisting of the fivefold chief and retinue in
front of an image, if you have one. The torma should be surrounded by pellets
and decorated with ornaments and a red silken canopy. Assemble an abundance of excellent foods, including fruits, meat, and wine. To the right and
left of these, place the amrita and rakta. In front, arrange the line of outer
offerings, the offering tormas, feast articles, and so forth. Sit facing the west for
practice.*

In the sky before me is the guru,
Indivisible from the Wisdom Dakini,
Vividly present in a form embodying all objects of refuge.

---

40 Translated by Erik Pema Kunsang

In the Wisdom Dakini, I take refuge!ᚖ
To swiftly attain buddhahood, I form the bodhichitta resolve!ᚖ

Repeat that three times.

Oᴍ ᴀʜ ʜᴜɴɢᚖ
The three realms, the vessel and contents, glory and riches,ᚖ
My body, luxuries, and all virtues,ᚖ
I offer to the lords of compassion.ᚖ
Accepting them, please bestow your blessings.ᚖ
Oᴍ ꜱᴀʀᴠᴀ ᴛᴀᴛʜᴀɢᴀᴛᴀ ʀᴀᴛɴᴀ ᴍᴀɴᴅᴀʟᴀ ᴘᴜᴊᴀ ʜᴏʜᚖ

By saying that, present the outer, inner, and innermost mandala offerings.

Pay heed, Guru Dakini, pay heed,ᚖ
With devotion, I supplicate you from my heart!ᚖ
Grant your blessings and dispel obstacles!ᚖ
Confer the four empowerments and bestow the siddhis!ᚖ
Oᴍ ᴀʜ ʜᴜɴɢ ᴍᴀʜᴀ ɢᴜʀᴜ ᴅᴀᴋɪɴɪ ꜱᴠᴀʜᴀᚖ

Accumulate as many of these as you can.

From the four places of the Guru Dakini,ᚖ
White, red, blue, and green rays of light radiate.ᚖ
As they dissolve into my four places,ᚖ
My four obscurations are purified, and I obtain the four
    empowerments.ᚖ
The guru, dissolving indivisibly into me,ᚖ
Becomes the luminous state of great bliss.ᚖ

These were the preliminary steps for gathering the accumulations.

Mᴀɪɴ Pᴀʀᴛ

Second, dispel the obstructors, saying,

Hʀɪʜᚖ
In the utterly pure mind essence,ᚖ

There is not even the term "deluded obstructors."
Within the space of the awakened mind of all phenomena,
The vajra protection circle is spontaneously perfected.
VAJRA RAKSHA RAKSHA HUNG

Bring down the resplendence and consecrate the offerings, saying,

The entire world is the dakini buddhafield.
All beings are the form of wisdom dakinis.
All the offering articles are the wisdom nectar of great bliss.
Outer, inner, and innermost offerings fill the sky.
OM SARVA PUJA MEGHA AH HUNG

Repeat (the mantra) three times.

Generate the deity, saying,

HRIH BHRUM DHUMA GHAYE NAMA SVAHA
Arising from the awakened mind,
What appears and exists is a buddhafield, the display of the
    dakinis.
Within the vajra protection circle,
Amidst the blazing triangular source-of-dharmas,
Upon the lotus, sun, and bamro,
I am the dakini Sangwa Yeshe.

Brilliant red, with one face and two arms,
I raise the curved knife, cutting through birth and death,
And hold the blood-filled skull cup, emptying samsara.
My three eyes gaze passionately.
I am in the full bloom of youth, like a sixteen-year-old,
With swelling breasts and my bhaga fully grown.

Between my eyes, the whorl-of-joy spins,
And my hair, black and shining, is tied up behind.
Adorned with a crown of five dried skulls,
I am decorated with the six bone ornaments.
With one leg bent and one extended, I stand in dancing pose,
Embracing the daka khatvanga,
Ablaze with boundless rays of red light.

In the four directions, upon four-petaled lotus flowers,§
Are the four dakinis of the four families, looking like me.§
In the brilliant hues of blue, yellow, white, and green,§
They hold curved knives with the attributes of their families.§
Surrounded by a hundred thousand dakinis of the sacred places
    and valleys,§
With the five wisdoms and body, speech, and mind,§
I am equal to all the victorious ones.§
Hrih hung tam om ah, om ah hung§

Invoke and dissolve the wisdom beings and make offerings and praises,
saying,

HRIH§
From the dharmadhatu beyond arising,§
And from the sambhogakaya realm beyond ceasing,§
Wisdom Dakini, together with your retinue,§
I invite you to this place; please come!§
Vajra samajah, e ah ralli hring hring§
Jah hung bam hoh, tishtha lhan, namo purushaya hoh§

HRIH§
From the union of the lord and lady, the world and all beings§
Are spontaneously perfected as the five sense pleasures.§
The union of means and knowledge§
Fills the sky with a cloud of innermost offerings.§

In nondual equality, I present§
This unexcelled, innermost offering§
Of the one taste of indivisible cognizance and emptiness,§
So enjoy it as the adornment of great bliss.§
MAHASUKHA PUJA HOH§

HRIH§
Dharmakaya, the state of emptiness,§
Sambhogakaya, luminous great bliss,§
Nirmanakaya, limitless variety of magical manifestations,§
I respectfully praise the hosts of dakinis.§

The recitation has three parts: approach, accomplishment, and activity. First, for the approach recitation, while possessing vivid presence, steady pride, and recollection of the pure symbolism, say,

> In my heart center, the syllable hrih rests upon a sun disc,
> Surrounded by the mantra garland, spinning anti-clockwise.
> Radiating light, it makes offerings to all the victorious ones,
> While gathering and absorbing their blessings and siddhis.
> It purifies the obscurations of beings throughout space
> And establishes them in the state of the wisdom dakini.
> As the rays of light are gathered back,
> They purify my obscurations and bestow blessings,
> And I become a suitable vessel for accomplishment.
> OM DHUMA GHAYE NAMA SVAHA

Recite this until you complete either a set number of recitations or a specified time period—or until a sign manifests. Next, for the accomplishment recitation, say,

> Amidst the dome of light in my heart center,
> Within the unchanging bindu, is Gargyi Wangchuk, the Lord of
>   the Dance.
> Brilliant red, he holds a lotus and the vase of longevity,
> Embracing his consort Dhatvishvari in union.
>
> From the cloud of bodhichitta of their union,
> A continuous garland of mantra appears.
> Passing through the body, it emerges from my nose,
> And the khatvanga turns into a daka.
>
> Entering his nose and passing through the throat
> To the tip of the vajra jewel,
> It spins like the wheel of a firebrand.
> Passing through the lotus, it dissolves into the heart.
>
> The rays of light of the bodhichitta
> Illuminate the entire world and all beings as a mandala.
> Light rays appear from the three places
> Of the deities, who fill the expanse of the sky.

Dissolving into me, they kindle the great bliss,ༀ
And I obtain the twofold accomplishment.ༀ

*Recite the mantra while visualizing this. Third, for the activity recitation,
which comes after having completed the approach and accomplishment, say,*

From the heart syllable of the wisdom being,ༀ
The radiating light makes the retinue devisༀ
Emanate innumerable replicas of themselves,ༀ
Fulfilling the four kinds of activity.ༀ
Hrih ma ha ri ni sa om bhrum hrih hungༀ

*Recite this one-tenth as much as the approach and accomplishment man-
tras. The particular activity-recitation should be learned from the root text.*

*During the session break, offer the Thousand Verses in the general way.
Or, if you prefer a slightly more elaborate way, arrange the offering torma,
amrita, and rakta. Sanctify them with* ram yam kham, *and recite* om ah
hung hrih *three times. Then make this offering by appending the following
to the approach-mantra, saying three times,*

Maha pancha amrita rakta balingta khakha khahiༀ

Hungༀ
Perfect conqueror, Vajra Dakini,ༀ
With five wisdoms and body, speech, and mindༀ
Fully perfected, chief of all dakinis,ༀ
Universal sovereign, lady of great strength,ༀ
Owner of all siddhis and activity,ༀ
Always residing in the celestial realms of Dharmadhatu and
    Akanishtaༀ
And in the land of Uddiyana,ༀ
Each of your many realms and bodily formsༀ
Has a hundred thousand dakinis.ༀ

For your manifestation of dances, surpassing thought,ༀ
There are a hundred thousand dakinis beyond change.ༀ
With your melodious voice pervading space,ༀ
There are a hundred thousand dakinis singing songs of purity.ༀ

Out of your thought-free space of the threefold emancipation,§
There are a hundred thousand dakinis of compassionate displays.§
From your abundant ornaments and qualities,§
There are a hundred thousand dakinis beyond the mind's grasp.§

Acting for the welfare of beings through the four activities,§
There are a hundred thousand dakinis spontaneously fulfilling
    them.§
Of the wisdom types and the ones carrying out activities,§
There are a hundred million dakinis in your retinue.§

All of you, enjoy these offerings§
Of amrita, rakta, and the torma of sense pleasures!§
Dispel the outer, inner, and innermost obstacles!§
Bestow the supreme and common siddhis!§
Swiftly fulfill the four activities!§

Offer this into the sky, accompanied by musical sounds of the small hand-drum and so forth.

Conclusion

Third, for the concluding steps, consecrate the feast articles, saying,

HRIH§
The vast bhandha of space§
Is filled with the nectar of awareness-wisdom.§
The offering clouds of bodhichitta gather§
And become the feast enjoyments of great bliss.§

Recite OM AH HUNG *three times. To invite the field of accumulation, say,*

HRIH§
From the twenty-four sublime places§
And from the eight great charnel grounds,§
I invite you, hosts of mother dakinis,§
Dancing and swaying in the poses of great bliss,§
Tinkling and jingling with ornaments and bells,§

Sounding the beat of your small hand-drums.
Please come immediately
To the gathering of yogis and yoginis!
VAJRA SAMAJAH

For the offering, apology, and deliverance offering, say,

HRIH
I present this outer offering of sense pleasures
To delight the body of the dakinis!
This offering of the union of great bliss
I present to the voice of the dakinis!

This offering of indivisible bliss and emptiness
I present to the mind of the dakinis!
I mend my samaya in the expanse of great bliss,
Apologize within nondual space,
And deliver the three poisons in the state of self-liberation;
So bestow the supreme and common siddhis!
Gana chakra puja hoh, samaya shuddhe ah,
Matram rudra maraya phat
KHA KHA KHAHI

Set ablaze the experience of great bliss, while enjoying the five sense plea-
sures, especially in combination with the secret conduct. As the samaya of eat-
ing, enjoy in the manner of inner pouring and burning. Gather the residual
and say,

OM AH HUNG HA HOH HRIH
These sense pleasures of the vajra samaya become a cloud of nectar
    filling the sky.

Then dedicate it, saying,

HRIH
Hosts of dakinis, with unending brilliance,
Out of the play of wisdom space,
Partake of these residual enjoyments
And fulfill the activities according to your promise!
DAKA DAKI BALINGTA KHAHI

Following this, replenish the offerings and repeat the offering and praise as above. When combining this with receiving the siddhis, say,

Hrih

In the essence mandala of bodhichitta,

Gathering of deities reveling in wisdom magic,

Without departing, remember your vajra samaya

And bestow blessings, empowerments, and siddhis!

At the end of the essence mantra append,

Kaya waka chitta siddhi phala hoh

To apologize for mistakes, say,

Hoh

Within the mandala of the Wisdom Dakini,

Among the offerings, samadhis, activities, and so forth,

In the innate state of luminosity, I apologize

For the mistakes I have committed through incorrectness.

A a a

If you have a shrine object, perform the general tenshuk for the guests of the feast, which is the request to remain as the shrine object. If not, make the request to depart. Next, dissolve and re-emerge as the self-visualization. Then dedicate, make aspirations, and recite verses of auspiciousness.

Like a rainbow vanishing into the sky,

The display of spontaneous presence dissolves into space.

The state of primordially pure suchness

Is left free of artifice, hope, and fear.

A a a

Hoh

In the mandala of the Wisdom Dakini,

Within unconditioned space, I dedicate

All acts of engaging in the secret meaning.

May the two obscurations be purified, may wisdom increase,

May we be victorious in the battle with the four maras,

And may buddhahood swiftly be attained!

Uttering this, enter your daily activities.

These are the progressive steps of the path, which support development and recitation. If you wish to train in the completion stages with and without marks, you should learn them from the terma root text.

Through this complete sadhana,
Which has few words, profound meaning, and all the necessary parts,
May all beings journey the excellent path to celestial realms
And attain mastery over all phenomena.

This composition of necessary sadhana parts, which support practice for me and others, was extracted from the terma root text and arranged as a reading method by Chimey Tennyi Yungdrung Lingpa Tsal (Jamgön Kongtrül Lodrö Thaye). May virtuous goodness increase!

Sangwa Yeshe Mandala

COMMENTARY ON THE FULFILLMENT OF ALL WISHES:

The Sadhana of Dakini Sangwa Yeshe

From the Essence Manual entitled
Plentiful Vase of Profound Instructions[41]

Orgyen Tobgyal Rinpoche

The practice we have here is the sadhana of the dakini Sangwa Yeshe. On page one, it says it is from the Treasure Vase of Profound Instructions, so that is the source of this sadhana. Before doing the actual sadhana, you should recite the Cloud Bank of Great Bliss, the Supplication to the Lineage of the Dakini Sangwa Yeshe from the Treasure Vase of Profound Instructions, which was written by the previous Neten Chokling Rinpoche, Pema Gyurme.

Right after that comes the *Fulfillment of All Wishes: The Sadhana of Dakini Sangwa Yeshe* from the essence manual entitled *Plentiful Vase of Profound Instructions,* which is a complete cycle of instructions.

After the opening verse, the small writing says that the sadhana has three parts: preparation, main part, and conclusion, as does almost every other sadhana.

First, in an auspicious place, on a day such as the tenth day of the waxing moon, arrange a dakini torma consisting of the fivefold chief and retinue in front of an image, if you have one. The torma should be surrounded by pellets and decorated with ornaments and a red silken canopy. Assemble an abundance of excellent foods including fruits, meat, and wine. To the right and left of these, place the amrita and rakta. In front, arrange the line of outer offerings, the offering tormas, feast articles, and so forth.

---

41 Translated by Erik Pema Kunsang

You should practice this in an auspicious place, beginning on an important day, like the tenth day of the waxing or waning part of the lunar calendar; the waxing is the tenth day, and the waning is the twenty-fifth day. For those who want to specifically do the dakini practice, what makes a place auspicious? Various types of auspicious places include ones that have a single huge tree, not a forest; a dome-shaped cave; sindura-colored (reddish-orange) water flowing, such as a river of that color; a bhaga-shaped cliff, and so forth.

Some of the indispensable ingredients to put on the shrine are a cowrie shell and a mirror. On the bottom of a cowrie [shell], you write HA RI NI SA. There is also a chakra for the life force of the dakinis, and Mipham Rinpoche described how to design one of those. It is also taught that if you always wear the cowrie [shell] and the mirror without taking them off, then even if you don't do the dakini practice, you'll still accomplish it.

When beginning the practice, sit facing west. Why face west? One reason is because Uddiyana is to the west. Another point is that this dakini is for magnetizing activity, which is also connected to the western direction. When monks chant the sutras, they're supposed to sit facing Shravasti, because the Buddha mainly resided there. Here, you are trying to accomplish this dakini, so you face west.

Recite once the visualization for the refuge, saying,

> In the sky before me is the guru,
> Indivisible from the Wisdom Dakini,
> Vividly present in a form embodying all objects of refuge.

Refuge and bodhichitta, as a matter of fact, only have a single sentence each:

> In the Wisdom Dakini, I take refuge!$\frac{8}{8}$
> To swiftly attain buddhahood, I form the bodhichitta resolve!$\frac{8}{8}$

Repeat these two lines three times. That means if you bring the meaning to mind, then it's okay to say them three times. If you say them without bringing the meaning to mind, you can repeat them a thousand times, but it won't help much.

The next four lines are for the offerings. They begin with *The three realms, the vessel and contents, glory and riches,* and so forth, and end with the mantra. Together with that, you visualize the outer, inner, and innermost ways of performing the mandala offering.

The next four lines plus the mantra comprise the guru yoga:

> Pay heed, Guru Dakini, pay heed,
> With devotion, I supplicate you from my heart!
> Grant your blessings and dispel obstacles!
> Confer the four empowerments and bestow the siddhis!
> OM AH HUNG MAHA GURU DAKINI SVAHA

You should accumulate as many repetitions of this as you possibly can. For example, when doing this practice on the twenty-fifth day of the month at my monastery, we chant the four lines three times, then the mantra a hundred times. While chanting the mantra, you imagine that in the sky before you is the dakini Sangwa Yeshe, indivisible from your root guru. Then, while chanting the mantra, you imagine that you receive the four empowerments.

The next six lines are the visualization for having received the empowerments:

> From the four places of the Guru Dakini,
> White, red, blue, and green rays of light radiate.
> As they dissolve into my four places,
> My four obscurations are purified, and I obtain the four
>   empowerments.
> The guru, dissolving indivisibly into me,
> Becomes the luminous state of great bliss.

Afterwards, remain briefly in that state of luminosity. These were the preliminary steps; in other words, this was the ngöndro.

Next you dispel obstructors by offering them the torma. First consecrate the torma, summon the obstructors, and then hand them the torma. There's a mantra for each of these steps, but according to the text, it's fine if you skip doing this. On the other hand, if you feel that there are obstructors and you need to do something to be rid of them, then you'd better do it.

The text reads,

Hrih:

In the utterly pure mind essence,:

There is not even the term "deluded obstructors.":

Within the space of the awakened mind of all phenomena:

The vajra protection circle is spontaneously perfected.:

Vajra raksha raksha hung:

Wouldn't it be sufficient to just understand the first two sentences, that the nature of mind is utterly pure? That means the mind is empty, right? And in the empty mind, how can there be any delusion? Even if there were an obstructor, it's just the play of this empty mind; it doesn't exist anywhere, really. If you bring this to mind and comprehend it, then how could there be an obstructing demon anywhere?

Understand that all obstructing demons are the play of our own minds; and within the space of the empty awakened mind of all phenomena, the vajra protection circle is actually already spontaneously perfected. Isn't it true that there's no protection greater than realizing emptiness? When you realize emptiness, even if the whole universe were to rise up as your enemy, it couldn't hurt you or inflict harm in any way. At the end of the verse you have the mantra, Vajra raksha raksha hung.

The next four lines are a combination of bringing down the resplendence and consecrating the offerings. The first two lines state,

The entire world is the dakini buddhafield.:

All beings are the form of wisdom dakinis.:

These two lines pertain to bringing down the resplendence. And the next two are the consecration.

All the offering articles are the wisdom nectar of great bliss.:

Outer, inner, and innermost offerings fill the sky.:

Om sarva puja megha ah hung:

From that perspective, you don't have to consecrate each, like the water, the flowers, the perfume, and so forth, because everything is an offering. Outer, inner, innermost phenomena, everything is an offering. When it says repeat three times, it refers to the mantra, om sarva puja

MEGHA AH HUNG. If you have musical instruments to play, then you sound them at this time.

The next mantra here, HRIH BHRUM DHUMA GHAYE NAMA SVAHA, is for manifesting the deity. In the *Light of Wisdom*, Volume II (*Lamrim Yeshe Nyingpo*) there is an Anuyoga-style development stage, where simply saying the mantra is enough for the complete visualization to unfold.

At this point, you visualize the deity, which is one central figure, with one goddess in each of the four directions.

> HRIH BHRUM DHUMA GHAYE NAMA SVAHA
> Arising from the awakened mind, ...
> I am equal to all the victorious ones.

That completes the visualization. Unlike other dakini practices, where they have red hair that blazes up, streaming upward, here it's black shining hair tied toward the back. Between the eyebrows, which are in the lower part of the forehead, at the spot where in India they put the *tika*, there is a design called the "whorl-of-joy." It is a delicate drawing, as if it were painted by a brush with a single hair, and it spins. Unlike Vajravarahi, Sangwa Yeshe has no pig's head. The khatvanga she holds signifies the daka, and the top of the khatvanga is a vajra, not a trident. Otherwise, she has one face, two arms, and so forth. There's no need to explain that part, as it is quite straightforward.

The visualization ends with a mantra, which is said while performing the corresponding mudras.

> HRIH HUNG TRAM OM AH, OM AH HUNG

For lotus-family deities, when you arrange the five syllables, the top one is HRIH, for Amitabha's family. Then, Akshobhya is at the forehead with his HUNG. TRAM for Ratnasambhava is at the right side, and in the back is OM for Vairocana. The AH here is for Amoghasiddhi. The OM AH HUNG for body, speech, and mind are the same as usual. When you do the mudras, they correspond to those places.

Invoke and dissolve the wisdom beings and make offerings and praises, saying,

As mentioned earlier, the chief figure, the samaya being that you visualize here, sends out rays of light from the heart center. The tips of the light rays bend slightly like hooks, for they go to the buddhafields, and especially to Dhumathala and the twenty-three other sacred places, to invoke and summon hundreds and thousands of forms of dakinis. These are the four lines of invocation:

> Hrih
> From the dharmadhatu beyond arising,
> And from the sambhogakaya realm beyond ceasing,
> Wisdom Dakini, together with your retinue,
> I invite you to this place; please come!
> Vajra samajah, e ah ralli hring hring
> Jah hung bam hoh, tishtha lhan, namo purushaya Hoh

In regard to the mantra, jah is to invite, hung is to make firm or remain, bam is to mingle indivisibly, and hoh is to enjoy. Tishtha lhan means "please remain"; and namo purushaya hoh is paying homage.

You chant this four-line invocation with a gentle melody, while playing the damaru. I asked Dilgo Khyentse Rinpoche whether this melody was from the Chokling Tersar tradition, and he said, "No, it isn't. It comes from Do Khyentse Yeshe Dorje." It's the invocation tune for the *Yumka Dechen Gyalmo* sadhana, according to *Longchen Nyingtig*. Whatever the case, they could in fact be the same tune.

The next eight lines include the outer, inner, innermost, and innermost secret offerings of *thatness:*

> Hrih
> From the union of the lord and lady, the world and all beings . . .
> So enjoy it as the adornment of great bliss.
> Mahasukha puja hoh

The next verse comprises the praises, where you say,

> Hrih
> Dharmakaya, the state of emptiness . . .
> I respectfully praise the host of dakinis.

*The recitation has three parts: approach, accomplishment, and activity.
First, for the approach recitation, while possessing vivid presence, steady
pride, and recollection of the pure symbolism, say,*

> In my heart center, the syllable HRIH rests upon a sun disc, . . .
> While gathering and absorbing their blessings and siddhis.
>
> It purifies the obscurations of beings throughout space, . . .
> And I become a suitable vessel for accomplishment.
> OM DHUMA GHAYE NAMA SVAHA

*Recite this until you complete either a set number of recitations or a spec-
ified time period—or until a sign manifests.*

The first four lines describe the visualization that you do while
chanting. For magnetizing and subjugating activity, such as this, the
mantra is written in a clockwise direction, but it faces inward toward
the seed syllable, rather than outward as in a typical yidam sadhana.
Also, the mantra then spins anti-clockwise rather than clockwise.

When doing a retreat, you should recite this approach mantra until
completing either a set number or a set period of time, or until a certain sign manifests. The set number, generally speaking, is one hundred
thousand mantras for each syllable in the mantra. But if the mantra is
shorter than twelve syllables, as in this case where the mantra has eight
syllables, then the number is larger. If it has many syllables, like the
Hundred Syllable mantra of Vajrasattva, then you don't need to repeat
it that many times. However, it's also said that since we're now in the
age of strife, we need to say a higher number than usual.

The set period of time refers to doing retreat for three months, six
months, or one year. According to the tantras, a six-month period is
quite a long time for a single sadhana.

As for signs, there are higher, medium, and lesser signs. The higher
sign is to have a vision of the deity in actuality and to hear the sound of
the mantra. The medium is to have a good meditation experience—not
like the feeling you get after taking a drug; not that kind of experience.
The lowest sign is to have excellent dreams.

For dakini practices, it is said that if you feel completely upset mentally and almost can't stay in the retreat the first few days, it's actually a very good sign for having some accomplishment from the practice. Dilgo Khyentse Rinpoche once did a five-month retreat on *Khandro Sangdü,* and he said that the first part of the retreat was almost unbearable. He thought, "I'm going nuts. I'm going insane." But whatever that meant, later on it turned out quite well. Also, when Trulshik Rinpoche was in Tibet in the early days, he did the previously mentioned Nyang terma of a dakini practice; he, too, had severe upheavals during the first part of his retreat. On the other hand, if you feel very serene, very calm, and so forth at the beginning, like a placid surface of an undisturbed lake, that means nothing beneficial is going to happen, and there will be no accomplishment either.

Next, for the accomplishment recitation, say,

> Amidst the dome of light in my heart center,
> Within the unchanging bindu, is Gargyi Wangchuk, the
>   lord of the dance. . . .
> And I obtain the twofold accomplishment.

Recite the mantra while visualizing this.

This needs a brief clarification. You, yourself, are Sangwa Yeshe, and in your heart center there is a dome. This doesn't look like the dome surrounding Vajrakilaya; rather, it's a sphere of red light. Inside of that is also a small sphere, not exactly a sphere, but it is the lord of the dance, Gargyi Wangchuk. He is a manifestation of Amitayus, and in essence is Avalokiteshvara. He's brilliant red, and in his two hands he's holding a lotus and a vase of longevity. He is in union with his consort, Dhatvishvari, and from their union appears a cloudbank of bodhichitta, which turns into a continuous mantra garland that passes through your body and then comes out through your nose. Sangwa Yeshe holds a khatvanga in the crook of her arm. When the mantra garland enters the khatvanga, that causes it to transform into the daka (male deity). The mantra garland then passes through his body and comes out through his vajra jewel, in a circle, just like a firebrand. It re-enters you as Sangwa Yeshe through the lotus and again dissolves back into the heart center.

The light rays that emanate from this illuminate the entire world as a mandala, meaning that all experiences are divine forms, all sounds are mantra, and all movement of mind is original wakefulness. This being so, deities appear filling all of space, and from their three places rays of light shine forth. These light rays dissolve into you, and through this the great bliss is kindled even further. Having set the great bliss ablaze, you have obtained the twofold siddhi. While visualizing this, you recite the same mantra as before: OM DHUMA GHAYE NAMA SVAHA.

Third, for the activity recitation, which comes after having completed the approach and accomplishment, say,

> From the heart syllable of the wisdom being,
> The radiating light makes the retinue devis
> Emanate innumerable replicas of themselves,
> Fulfilling the four kinds of activity.
> HRIH MA HA RI NI SA OM BHRUM HRIH HUNG

Recite this one-tenth as much as the approach and accomplishment man-tras. The particular activity-recitation should be learned from the root text.

In this mantra, OM is for pacifying; BHRUM is for increasing; HRIH is for magnetizing; HUNG is for subjugating. You recite it one-tenth as much as the main mantra. So, if you've done one million of the approach and accomplishment mantras, then you would do one hundred thousand of this mantra. If you are only doing the practice for the twenty-fifth day feast offering, then you just do as many as you see fit.

The particular activity-recitation has something to do with Kurukulle, and in the terma root text, there's also a longevity practice.

During the session break, offer the Thousand Verses in the general way. Or, if you prefer a slightly more elaborate way, arrange the offering torma, amrita, and rakta. Sanctify them with RAM YAM KHAM, *and recite* OM AH HUNG HRIH *three times. Then make this offering by appending the following to the approach-mantra, saying three times,*

MAHA PANCHA AMRITA RAKTA BALINGTA KHAKHA KHAHI

The Thousand Verses mentioned here include the Vowels and Consonants (*ali-kali*), repeating the offerings and praises, and then the Hundred Syllable mantra.

If you prefer to practice in a slightly more elaborate way, then you can perform a torma offering. The torma offering is actually a very important part, and the torma to the dakinis, made of flesh and blood, should not be interrupted—don't miss a single day. The torma has a particular design with a main peak and five smaller peaks. If you don't have this special flesh-and-blood torma, then you can offer a small piece of beef and grapes or other red fruits, together with some red flowers and wine. To do this, first sanctify the torma offering with RAM YAM KHAM and then OM AH HUNG HRIH three times. You then make the offering by saying the approach mantra with the offering mantra added at the end, like so: OM DHUMA GHAYE NAMA SVAHA MAHA PANCHA AMRITA RAKTA BALINGTA KHA-KHA KHAHI. Then offering the torma, you say,

> HUNG
> Perfect conqueror, Vajra Dakini, . . .
> Each of your many realms and bodily forms
> Has a hundred thousand dakinis. . . .
>
> Of the wisdom types and the ones carrying out activities,
> There are a hundred million dakinis in your retinue.

Offer this into the sky, accompanied by musical sounds of the small hand-drum, and so forth.

This is called the *Hundred Thousand Dakini Song*, and it is found in many different texts, in both the Nyingma Kama and original Terma scriptures. You find the same wording in the *Chakrasamvara* sadhana.

The small hand-drum mentioned in the small writing is not a damaru, but a different kind of small instrument, like ones you see in India sometimes. Jigme Lingpa provides a detailed description of how to make one in his explanation of the *Gongdü*, and if you make that particular type of hand-drum, then definitely all the dakinis will arrive as soon as you play it.

Accompanied by this music, you offer the torma into the sky. If you place the torma offering for the dakinis in a place where human beings, dogs, and other scavengers can get to it, there will be severe repercussions. In other words, don't just throw it up in the air and let it fall down on the ground, but place it somewhere out of harm's way.

Next is the third part, the conclusion. First, for the feast, consecrate the feast articles, saying,

> HRIH
> The vast bhandha of space . . .

Recite OM AH HUNG three times.

The vast bhandha of space refers to inner space of the body itself. *Filled with the nectar of awareness wisdom* is easy to understand. The expression of awareness (*rigpa'i tsal*) is called *cloud of bodhichitta*. Whenever the expression of awareness is allowed to be spontaneously liberated within the expanse of emptiness, it is called *the feast enjoyments of great bliss.*

Then comes the invocation.

To invite the field of accumulation, say,

> HRIH
> From the twenty-four sublime places
> And from the eight great charnel grounds,
> I invite you, hosts of mother dakinis,
> Dancing and swaying in the poses of great bliss,
> Tinkling and jingling with ornaments and bells,
> Sounding the beat of your small hand drums,
> Please come immediately
> To the gathering of yogis and yoginis!
> VAJRA SAMAJAH

The twenty-four sublime places have external locations, but they also correspond to locations within the body. When I looked for the geographical locations of these twenty-four places, I was only able to figure out eight of them, and in each of those places there is a Hindu temple with a shrine for Maheshvara. The eight great charnel grounds are *the Cool Grove* in India, the one in Nepal, if that is counted among them; otherwise, I don't know the others. The dakinis live in those places, and you invite them from there. Uddiyana is also counted among the twenty-four places. The inner twenty-four places within our body are exactly as they are explained in the *Yumka* of the Longchen Nyingtig.[42]

When the dakinis arrive, they dance like belly-dancers, jingling and tinkling and playing small hand drums, inviting all yogis and yoginis to join the gathering. It's said that there must be both yogis and yoginis; otherwise, the dakinis won't come. *Come immediately* means, "right this moment." VAJRA SAMAJAH.

Next are the offering, the apology, and the deliverance, together in one chant.

For the offering, apology, and deliverance offering, say,

HRIH:
I present this outer offering of sense pleasures:
To delight the body of the dakinis!:
This offering of the union of great bliss:
I present to the voice of the dakinis!: . . .
And deliver the three poisons in the state of self-liberation;:
So bestow the supreme and common siddhis!:
GANA CHAKRA PUJA HOH, SAMAYA SHUDDHE AH,:
MATRAM RUDRA MARAYA PHAT:

Set ablaze the experience of great bliss while enjoying the five sense pleasures, especially in combination with the secret conduct. As the samaya of eating, enjoy in the manner of inner pouring and burning.

Except for monks, everybody is probably well aware of what the *secret conduct* is. To *enjoy in the manner of inner pouring and burning* means the inner heat has been set ablaze, so that consuming food and drink ignites the flames even further, and the pure part of the essences are then offered to the deities, who naturally abide within the channels and the chakras. After that, gather the residuals. To consecrate them say,

OM AH HUNG HA HOH HRIH:
These sense pleasures of the vajra samaya become a cloud of nectar
filling the sky.:

Then dedicate it, saying,

HRIH:

Hosts of dakinis, with unending brilliance,°
Out of the play of wisdom space,°
Partake of these residual enjoyments°
And fulfill the activities according to your promise!°
Daka daki balingta khahi°

The residual offering is not for the wisdom dakini, but for the manifestations of the wisdom dakini—mainly what are called the twenty-eight ishvaris, or *wangchukmas* in Tibetan.

Following this, replenish the offerings and repeat offering and praise as above. When combining this with receiving the siddhis, say,

Hrih°
In the essence mandala of bodhichitta,°
Gathering of deities reveling in wisdom magic,°
Without departing, remember your vajra samaya°
And bestow blessings, empowerments, and siddhis!°

And then *at the end of the essence mantra,* om ah hung maha guru dakini svaha, add kaya waka chitta siddhi phala hoh.°

To apologize for mistakes say,

Hoh°
Within the mandala of the Wisdom Dakini,°
Among the offerings, samadhis, activities, and so forth,°
In the innate state of luminosity, I apologize°
For the mistakes I've committed through incorrectness.°
A a a°

If you have a shrine object, perform the general tenshuk for the guests of the feast, which is the request for them to remain as shrine objects.

The general way to do that is to recite the short verse beginning with *Dirni tendang lhenchig du.* You'll likely always have a shrine object, but if not, then you don't chant this.

Next, dissolve and re-emerge as the self-visualization. Then dedicate, make aspirations, and recite verses of auspiciousness.

Like a rainbow vanishing into the sky,§
The display of spontaneous presence dissolves into space.§
The state of primordially pure suchness§
Is left free of artifice, hope, and fear.§
A A A§

Just as a rainbow vanishes into the sky, the spontaneous presence, which is the mandala of the deity that manifested out of primordial purity, is now effortlessly allowed to dissolve back into the state of primordial purity. Just leave it be, without artifice, without hope or fear. This is different than normal dissolution, where you first dissolve the realm into the palace, the palace into the surrounding deities, and the deities into the central figure, which then slowly disappears. Here, it all happens at once of its own accord. Finally, you say,

Hoh§
In the mandala of the Wisdom Dakini,§
Within unconditioned space, I dedicate§
All acts of engaging in the secret meaning.§
May the two obscurations be purified, may wisdom increase,§
May we be victorious in the battle with the four maras,§
And may buddhahood swiftly be attained!§

Uttering this, enter your daily activities.

These are the progressive steps of the path, which support development and recitation. If you wish to train in the completion stages with and without marks, you should learn them from the terma root text.

There's also a verse of auspiciousness from the previous Chokling Rinpoche, which you can include if you would like to chant more verses of auspiciousness.

This explains the basic framework for the sadhana. However, on the twenty-fifth day, it would be excellent if you also include the longevity practice. After you have done the approach, accomplishment, and activity-recitation, then insert the recitation for longevity. There's also a particular fire puja to add in at some point, which pertains to the activities. All the masters say if you want a dakini practice that is simple, effective, and easy to apply, then this is it.

Among the six cycles of the *Zurza Tukdam,* there is an arrangement of the Yeshe Tsogyal practice made by the second Chokling incarnation (the same one who wrote the ngöndro text entitled *The Great Gate*), which is also very good to do on the twenty-fifth day, but sometimes people feel it's a little too long.

We'll stop here. Sometimes, if you say too much about the dakinis, they get upset.

Sangwa Yeshe & Gargyi Wangchuk

COMMENTARY ON THE FULFILLMENT OF ALL WISHES[43]

Lama Putsi Pema Tashi[44]

PREPARATION

In the sky before me is the guru,
Indivisible from the Wisdom Dakini,
Vividly present in a form embodying all objects of refuge.

In front of you is the root guru who has pointed out your mind as
dharmakāya, indivisible from the wisdom Dākinī Sangwa Yeshe, the
embodiment of all objects and sources of refuge—of the Three Roots and
Three Jewels, present as the embodiment of the Three Roots. Visualizing in this way, take refuge in the wisdom Dākinī Sangwa Yeshe, until
attaining the heart of awakening, by saying,

In the Wisdom Dakini, I take refuge!§
To swiftly attain buddhahood, I form the bodhichitta resolve!§

Repeat that three times.

In order to bring all beings living in the three realms of cyclic existence to the level of buddhahood, you practice the profound path and set
your resolve on buddhahood in aspiration and application. This is how to
form your resolve. Then continue with the preliminaries.

OM AH HUNG§ . . .
The three realms, the vessel and contents, glory and riches,§
My body, luxuries, and all virtues,§
I offer to the lords of compassion.§

---

43 Translated by Zack Beer and Marcia B. Schmidt

Accepting them, please bestow your blessings.⸭
Oᴍ sᴀʀᴠᴀ ᴛᴀᴛʜᴀɢᴀᴛᴀ ʀᴀᴛɴᴀ ᴍᴀɴᴅᴀʟᴀ ᴘᴜᴊᴀ ʜᴏʜ⸭

This is the offering of the outer, inner, and secret mandala, just as in the *Tukdrub* preliminary practices and elsewhere.

> *By saying that, present the outer, inner, and innermost mandala offerings.*

Next is guru yoga, where you supplicate,

> Pay heed, Guru Dakini, pay heed,⸭ . . .
> Confer the four empowerments and bestow the siddhis!⸭
> Oᴍ ᴀʜ ʜᴜɴɢ ᴍᴀʜᴀ ɢᴜʀᴜ ᴅᴀᴋɪɴɪ sᴠᴀʜᴀ⸭

Accumulate as much of this mantra as you can. *Pay heed, kye* in Tibetan, is a phrase of calling out. You supplicate the wisdom Dākinī Sangwa Yeshe, indivisible from your own root guru, with devotion from the heart. Thus, your body, speech, and mind are blessed by awakened body, speech, and mind. You are beseeching her to dispel temporary and ultimate obstacles to your practice of the sacred dharma. Please confer the four empowerments—the vase, secret, knowledge, and word empowerments—and bestow the siddhis. Thus, having supplicated, you chant the mantra Oᴍ ᴀʜ ʜᴜɴɢ ᴍᴀʜᴀ ɢᴜʀᴜ ᴅᴀᴋɪɴɪ sᴠᴀʜᴀ as much as you can. This is the guru yoga preliminary. You have requested the bestowal of the four empowerments from the guru Dākinī with the words *Confer the four empowerments*. So, after accumulating the mantra, you take the actual empowerment:

> From the four places of the Guru Dakini,⸭
> White, red, blue, and green rays of light radiate.⸭

Lights radiate from the four places—the crown, throat, heart, and navel—of your root guru as inseparable from the wisdom Dākinī Sangwa Yeshe. As it is said, "From oᴍ at the crown of the head, white light radiates and dissolves into the crown of your head, whereby you receive the vase empowerment." Similarly, with the visualization of the other empowerments, red light radiates from the throat and dissolves into your throat, blue light issues from the heart and merges into your heart, and green light emanates from the navel, melting into your navel.

> As they dissolve into my four places,§
> My four obscurations are purified, and I obtain the four
>   empowerments.§

Thus, as it is said, when you receive the fourth empowerment, the obscurations to wisdom are purified, and you are empowered to practice the Great Perfection. Light emanates four times, flowing into your four places, purifying the four obscurations, and endowing you with the vase, secret, wisdom-knowledge, (and word) empowerments.

> The guru, dissolving indivisibly into me,§
> Becomes the luminous state of great bliss.§

Finally, the guru joyfully melts into light and dissolves into you, and you settle in evenness *(nyamzhag),* indivisible from the guru. Resting in a state of luminous great bliss, free from all conceptual elaboration, think that your mind has merged indivisibly with the guru. This is the same as when you settle in evenness (doing meditation practice), isn't it? Look into the natural face of dharmakaya.

MAIN PART

> HRIH§
> In the utterly pure mind essence,§
> There is not even the term "deluded obstructors."§
> Within the space of the awakened mind of all
>   phenomena,§
> The vajra protection circle is spontaneously perfected.§
> VAJRA RAKSHA RAKSHA HUNG§

These lines really seem to be following the intention of the Great Perfection. They are talking about mind's essence *(sems nyid)*—the true nature of mind—not mind, which is endowed with deluded thoughts of subject-object duality. Here it is mind essence, which has been pointed out to you; it is not that you have been introduced to mind mixed with deluded thoughts of subject-object duality, right? Obscurations have never penetrated the nature of mind, whose very identity is to be primordially free from all conceptual elaboration. In this originally pure ground of mind essence, pure from the beginning, there is not even the phrase *deluded obstructors*. In originally pure mind nature that is recognized, the root of the obstructors, subject-object delusion, does not exist. In recognition, there is not even the name.

The reason why this delusion doesn't exist is then described by the line that reads, *Within the space of the awakened mind of all phenomena.* The space of awakened mind is purified (*byang ba*) in being primordially untainted by defects and perfected (*chub pa*) in that all qualities are spontaneously present. That is how the space of awakened mind is. As it says in the *Tukdrub Gyepa*, "HUNG! *The Three Roots of the bodhichitta of natural awareness, Do not exist anywhere other than in the state indivisible from myself."*[45] Likewise, as it says in the *Treasury of Dharmadhātu,* "Primordially untainted by impurity, purified of samsara, perfected with spontaneously present qualities . . .". Thus, phenomena are the space of awakened mind, and awareness, the essence of the blissful ones, is empty in essence, cognizant in nature, and all-pervasive in capacity.

Within that space, *The vajra protection circle is spontaneously perfected.* Here to explain *vajra,* a material vajra is uncuttable, indestructible, real, solid, firm, and utterly unobstructed. This is the intrinsic vajradharma. Nothing else can destroy it, yet it has the power to annihilate everything else. Vajra is explained like that: Subject and object, all concepts about the characteristics of things, cannot split it; however, it can cut subject and object, all concepts about the characteristics of things. Meditating like that, you experience it to be present in a spontaneously perfected manner. VAJRA RAKSHA RAKSHA HUNG is the mantra for the protection circle.

Bring down the resplendence and consecrate the offerings, saying,

The entire world is the dakini buddhafield.
All beings are the form of wisdom dakinis.

Everything here is explained in terms of the Great Perfection: The entirety of the externally appearing vessel of the world, without exception, is a field of wisdom Dākinīs, pure like the western pure realm of Sukhāvatī. From all directions, light rays radiate, proliferating representations [of enlightened body, speech, and mind]. It is like this, replete with the features of a pure realm. The entire inner contents, the sentient beings, such as humans and animals, are manifest in the form of wisdom dakinis.

> All the offering articles are the wisdom nectar of great bliss.ᵉ
> Outer, inner, and innermost offerings fill the sky.ᵉ

All material things, the offering articles as well as all external things and implements, are the *wisdom nectar of great bliss. Outer, inner, and innermost offerings fill the sky.* As it is said, outer, inner, and innermost offerings are the great offering-seal of appearance and existence as manifest ground. The phrase *appearance and existence as manifest ground* encompasses all phenomena—here represented by the torma vessel of the apparent world, which holds the torma of the inner contents of all existent beings. To say appearance and existence are primordially manifest as the ground indicates that all phenomena are inherently pure from the beginning. Even the word *impure* is irrelevant. So outer, inner, and innermost offerings fill the sky. Offering clouds are indicated by the mantra, where you say,

> Oᴍ sᴀʀᴠᴀ ᴘᴜᴊᴀ ᴍᴇɢʜᴀ ᴀʜ ʜᴜɴɢᵉ

Repeat (the mantra) three times.

Then you develop the deity, saying,

> Hʀɪʜ ʙʜʀᴜᴍ ᴅʜᴜᴍᴀ ɢʜᴀʏᴇ ɴᴀᴍᴀ sᴠᴀʜᴀᵉ

As the mantra of the definitive, luminous ground, ʜʀɪʜ is the root syllable for the magical display. Hʀɪʜ ʙʜʀᴜᴍ ᴅʜᴜᴍᴀ ɢʜᴀʏᴇ ɴᴀᴍᴀ sᴠᴀʜᴀ is the mantra for developing the deity. All mantras are unmistaken wisdom, and this wisdom within the mantras provides the conditions for developing the deity and enacting the noble activities. For example, the mantra for Vajrakilaya, oᴍ ʙᴇɴᴢᴀ ᴋɪʟɪ ᴋɪʟᴀʏᴀ, is the mantra for developing that deity with the name of Dorje Shonnu, Vajrakilaya.

> Arising from the awakened mind,ᵉ
> What appears and exists is a buddhafield, the display of the
>   dakinis.ᵉ
> Within the vajra protection circle,ᵉ

Generally, the development phase can unfold according to Anu or Ati. If you are developing HRIH BHRUM DHUMA GHAYE NAMA SVAHA, according to Anu, then, with the mantra for developing you should think, "Everything is the nature of deity and the buddhafield." You plant the stakes of the three samadhis with this development mantra.

Awakened mind is the ground, the buddha nature, which is not tainted or obscured but pure from the beginning. From this pure ground, everything that appears and exists is the buddhafield. All of existence, the container and the contents, is the display of the Ḍākinī buddhafield. The entire deity visualization is within this protection circle of the three vajras.

> Amidst the blazing triangular source-of-dharmas,⁰
> Upon the lotus, sun, and bamro,⁰
> I am the dakini Sangwa Yeshe,⁰ . . .
> Embracing the daka khatvanga,⁰
> Ablaze with boundless rays of red light.⁰

This daka khatvanga is her consort, who is Padmasambhava. The top of the khatvanga has a vjara, which is the yab, the method.

> In the four directions, upon four-petaled lotus flowers,⁰
> Are the four dakinis of the four families, looking like me.⁰

The main figure is Sangwa Yeshe and the retinue is in the four directions.

> In the brilliant hues of blue, yellow, white, and green,⁰
> They hold curved knives with the attributes of their families.⁰

The blue vajra khandro in the east has a vajra [on top of the knife], the yellow ratna khandro in the south has a jewel, the white buddha khandro in the west has a wheel, and the green karma khandro in the north has a crossed vajra.

> Surrounded by a hundred thousand dakinis of the sacred places
>   and valleys,⁰

This refers to the twenty–four sacred places and the thirty-two valleys.

With the five wisdoms and vajra body, speech, and mind,⁞
I am equal to all the victorious ones.⁞

This is empowering you with the five wisdoms and sealing that with enlightened body, speech, and mind, which makes you equal to the victorious ones.

Hᴙɪʜ ʜᴜɴɢ ᴛʀᴀᴍ ᴏᴍ ᴀʜ, ᴏᴍ ᴀʜ ʜᴜɴɢ⁞

You are empowered by the victorious ones. From your heart center, light rays emanate to invite the victorious ones and their retinues to appear in the space in front. From the place of illusory manifestations, they appear. The magical display blesses your own body, speech, and mind. Then, the lord of the family, Amitabha, truly manifests his wisdom: a white ᴏᴍ in the ushnisha, a red ᴀʜ in the throat, and a blue ʜᴜɴɢ in the heart center. Oᴍ ᴀʜ ʜᴜɴɢ, enlightened body, speech, and mind, bless your own body, speech, and mind, which are primordially the essence of the enlightened body, speech, and mind. This being so, it truly happens, and you are sealed by the three vajras; this is the sealing.

Next is the invitation.

Invoke and dissolve the wisdom beings, and make offerings and praises, saying,

Hʀɪʜ⁞
From the dharmadhatu beyond arising,⁞
And from the sambhogakaya realm beyond ceasing,⁞
Wisdom Dakini, together with your retinue,⁞
I invite you to this place; please come!⁞

From the dharmadhatu beyond arising, the seed syllable in your heart radiates infinite light rays and pervades the buddhafield with red rays like hooks. They invoke Sangwa Yeshe and her retinue of hundreds of thousands of Dākinīs to appear within the celestial palace in the sky before you. And from the sambhogakaya realm beyond ceasing means the wisdom appearances are completely free from arising, dwelling, and ceasing. They arise from the unborn dharmadhatu, the dharmakaya, free from elaborations. Their unobstructed, self-luminous [nature] is the sambhogakaya buddhafield. From this, the nirmanakaya wisdom Dākinī

Sangwa Yeshe and her retinue arise when you invoke them, saying, Wisdom Dakini, together with your retinue, I invite you to this place, please come!

This is the invitation.

VAJRA SAMAJAH, E AH RALLI HRING HRING
JAH HUNG BAM HOH, TISHTHA LHAN, NAMO PURUSHAYA HOH

Indivisibly, the mandala of the wisdom being dissolves into the samaya being, like water into water, and takes a seat.

From your heart center, inconceivable numbers of offering goddesses are emanated, offering prostrations.

HRIH
From the union of the lord and lady, the world and all beings
Are spontaneously perfected as the five sense pleasures.
The union of means and knowledge
Fills the sky with a cloud of innermost offerings.

These are exactly Dzogchen dharma words. From the union of the lord and lady, the world and all beings, means that the outer vessel of the world and the inner contents of its beings arise from the union of the male and female. To explain, the male and female represent space and awareness in union. Space is free from all elaborations; the subject is rigpa wisdom. To give the male a name, it is "wisdom." The line stating, *Are spontaneously perfected as the five sense pleasures,* means that primordially, all the various sense objects—sights, sounds, smells, toucheables, and so forth—are spontaneously perfected. Realizing the object, space free from elaborations, and recognizing the wisdom, the subject, to be free from elaborations is *the union of means and knowledge that fills up the sky with a cloud of innermost offerings.*

In nondual equality, I present
This unexcelled, innermost offering
Of the one taste of indivisible cognizance and emptiness,
So enjoy it as the adornment of great bliss.
MAHASUKHA PUJA HOH

Of the one taste of indivisible cognizance and emptiness, indicates that the empty essence and the cognizant nature are the inseparability of empty cognizance. Whatever appears is the nature of cognizance, and the essence of cognizance is empty. The cognizance arises from within the state of emptiness. Hence, indivisible empty cognizance is of one taste. In nondual equality, I present this unexcelled, innermost offering, means that you offer this without holding onto duality. Realizing the equality, or one taste, of samsara and nirvana, you are making the great bliss offering, mahasukha puja hoh, which can be enjoyed as the adornment of great bliss.

HRIH⁀

Dharmakaya, the state of emptiness,⁀

There are three kayas, dharmakaya, sambhogakaya, and nirmanakaya. Dharmakaya, the state of emptiness, means that within dharmakaya, all obscurations and habitual tendencies [are purified]. Resting in this state is the ultimate method for attaining buddhahood. Buddha nature is purified and perfected, as the two purities.[46] Possessing the twofold purity is called dharmakaya.

Sambhogakaya, luminous great bliss,⁀
Nirmanakaya, limitless variety of magical manifestations,⁀
I respectfully praise the hosts of dakinis.⁀

From within emptiness, free from all elaborations, dharmakaya emanates outwardly. The luminosity is the sambhogakaya, which unfolds from the dharmakaya, as the nature of luminous great bliss. Dharmakaya can be likened to clouds, and sambhogakaya activity can be likened to rain coming from these clouds. Bodhisattvas on the tenth bhumi can recognize the sambhogakaya and svabhavikakaya. From that, the nirmanakaya has the capacity to arise in a limitless variety of magical manifestations, to benefit and liberate impure sentient beings. Thus, wisdom Dākinī Sangwa Yeshe and her retinue manifest to tame beings.

Offering goddesses emanate from your heart center to offer prostrations and praises. Then these inconceivable offering goddesses dissolve back into your heart center.

The recitation has three parts: approach, accomplishment, and activity. . . .

Next, for the accomplishment-recitation, say,

> Amidst the dome of light in my heart center,ᵉ
> Within the unchanging bindu, is Gargyi Wangchuk, the lord of the
> dance.ᵉ

This is the jnana sattva.

> ... And I obtain the twofold accomplishment.ᵉ

Recite the mantra while visualizing this.

Third, for the activity-recitation, which comes after having completed the approach and accomplishment, say,

> From the heart syllable of the wisdom being,ᵉ
> The radiating light makes the retinue devisᵉ
> Emanate innumerable replicas of themselves,ᵉ
> Fulfilling the four kinds of activity.ᵉ

From the heart center of the wisdom being, Gargi Wangchuk, inconceivable light rays radiate and strike Sangwa Yeshe's four female retinue deities, who are dark blue, yellow, white, and green. They then Emanate innumerable replicas of themselves. When the light rays touch the heart of the vajra Dākinī, she sends out emanations that pacify sickness, malevolent spirits, the eight fears, and so forth. Light rays then dissolve back into you, and you accomplish the pacifying activity. Next, light rays strike the heart of the ratna Dākinī, who sends out inconceivable emanations and re-emanations. [She sends out light rays] that help beings achieve long life, merit, splendor, wealth, fame, and so forth in this world. As these yellow light rays dissolve back into you, think that you have accomplished the increasing activity. For the magnetizing activity, the great bliss, light rays from the White Dakini, who is Kurukulle, radiate inconceivably, accomplishing all the glory, wealth, and so forth of this world, which then dissolves into you. Think that you've now accomplished the magnetizing activity. Once again, light rays emanate from the heart center and hit the green deva, the karma Dākinī. From her heart center, infinite emanations and re-emanations exude. In the world, any person who has all ten negative characteristics, [samaya] violators, evil spirits, and all uncontrollable beings are liberated. The light rays then dissolve into you, and you think that the wrathful activity has been accomplished. In this way, think that the four kinds of activities are fulfilled.

HRIH MA HA RI NI SA OM BHRUM HRIH HUNG

To explain the mantra: HRIH MA, are the syllables of the male and female, HA RI NI SA, are the four classes of dakinis, OM BHRUM HRIH HUNG, are the syllables for the four activities.

Recite this one-tenth as much as the approach and accomplishment mantras. The particular activity-recitation should be learned from the root text.

During the session break, offer the Thousand Verses in the general way. Or, if you prefer a slightly more elaborate way, arrange the offering torma, amrita, and rakta. Sanctify them with RAM YAM KHAM, *and recite* OM AH HUNG HRIH *three times. Then make this offering by appending the following to the approach-mantra, saying three times,*

Maha pancha amrita rakta balingta khakha khahi . . .

CONCLUSION

HRIH
The vast bhandha of space
Is filled with the nectar of awareness-wisdom.
The offering clouds of bodhichitta gather,
And become the feast enjoyments of great bliss. . . .

If you have a shrine object, perform the general tenshuk for the guests of the feast, which is the request to remain as the shrine object. If not, make the request to depart. Next, dissolve and re-emerge the self-visualization. Then dedicate, make aspirations, and recite verses of auspiciousness.

Like a rainbow vanishing into the sky,
The display of spontaneous presence dissolves into space.
The state of primordially pure suchness
Is left free of artifice, hope, and fear.
AA A

Hoн:

In the mandala of the Wisdom Dakini,:

Within unconditioned space, I dedicate:

All acts of engaging in the secret meaning.:

May the two obscurations be purified, may wisdom increase,:

May we be victorious in the battle with the four maras,:

And may buddhahood swiftly be attained!:

Uttering this, enter your daily activities.

CLOUD BANKS OF BLESSINGS[47]

Supplication to the Lineage Gurus for the
Daily Practice of Yeshe Tsogyal

Chokgyur Dechen Lingpa

Primordial protector, great consort of Samantabhadra,
Five Dhatvishvari queens endowed with the five perfections,
Vajravarahi, who appears as the nirmanakaya,
I supplicate you; grant me the wisdom of great bliss!

Lord of Secrets and Dakini Leykyi Wangmo,
Padmasambhava and Yeshe Tsogyal,
Yeshe Rolpa Tsal and Princess Metok of Zur,
I supplicate you; grant me the wisdom of great bliss!

Root guru, vidyadhara, and your consort,
Wisdom dakinis, assemblage of mandala deities,
Dakas and dakinis, ocean of vow-holders,
I supplicate you; grant me the wisdom of great bliss!

Grant your blessings to perfect the development stage through the
    outer sadhana of Tara!
Grant your blessings to be adept in nadi and prana through the
    inner sadhana of Varahi!
Grant your blessings to realize the innate great bliss
Through the secret sadhana, the phonya path of Secret Wisdom!

Grant your blessings to attain mastery over immortality by
    undertaking asceticism
Through the innermost sadhana of Mandarava!
Grant your blessings to accomplish the wisdoms of the four visions
Through the thatness sadhana of Yeshe Tsogyal!

---

47 Translated by Erik Pema Kunsang

In response to encouragements from Dechen Chödrön, who possesses the transmission of this teaching, from the most faithful Jetsun Losang Chödrön, and others, as well as for the sake of the terma, I, Chokgyur Dechen Lingpa, composed this in Glorious Lhasa, the assembly place of dakinis, and Pema Rangdröl wrote it down.

ZURZA KHANDRO LINEAGE
SUPPLICATION COMMENTARY[48]

Tulku Urgyen Rinpoche

First you chant the lineage prayer. The primordial protector is Samantabhadra and his consort Samantabhadri. As soon as you say, "endowed with the five perfections, or certainties," that means the sambhogakaya. Here it is the five consorts of the five buddhas. The nirmanakaya is Vajravarahi. Bestow the wisdom of great bliss means great bliss is without even the word suffering. In the state of great bliss without grasping, there is wisdom, wakefulness. The Lord of Secrets is the same as Vajrapani, and Dakini Leykyi Wangmo is the compiler of the tantras. She is one of the gurus of Padmakara, whose consort is Yeshe Tsogyalma. Yeshe Rolpa Tsal is the past life of Chokgyur Lingpa. Princess Metok of Zur later incarnated as the consort of Chokgyur Lingpa, Dechen Chödrön. I supplicate you, bestow the wisdom of great bliss.

Root guru, vidyadhara and your consort, means Chokgyur Lingpa and his consort. The next line, Wisdom dakinis assemblage of mandala deities, refers to the deities in the sadhana here. The following line indicates dakas and the ocean of protectors.

Next it explains the different levels of sadhana. Through the outer sadhana of Tara, you perfect the development stage. The inner sadhana, which is Vajravarahi, makes the nadis and prana supple. The secret sadhana, which is Sangwa Yeshe, is the phonya path, whose practices relate to the third empowerment. By means of the example wisdom, you realize the ultimate wisdom, the true meaning. Please bestow the blessings to realize the innate great bliss.

Bestow your blessings to attain mastery over immortal longevity by undertaking asceticism. Once you apply the yogic discipline, you realize the deathless mastery of longevity, the vidyadhara level of immortal life.

---

48 Translated by Marcia B. Schmidt

The innermost sadhana, which is Mandarava, refers to the pith instructions. She was the princess of the king of Zahor. There are four sadhanas now, the outer, inner, secret, and innermost. There is lastly, the ultimate or the thatness sadhana, which is Yeshe Tsogyal, who is a Tibetan girl. Bestow your blessings to accomplish the wisdoms of the four visions.

The colophon reads, In response to encouragements from Dechen Chödrön, Chokgyur Lingpa's consort. She is the one who asked for this and is the recipient of the teachings and the holder of the lineage. She received it from the most faithful Jetsun Losang Chödrön, a nun and the daughter of a high dignitary, an assistant of the Dalai Lama. They asked many times and made many offerings. In response to them and many others, as well as for the sake of the terma, this was composed by Chokgyur Dechen Lingpa at Glorious Lhasa, the assembly place of dakinis, and written down by Pema Rangdröl.

Zurza Khandro

THE DAILY PRACTICE OF YESHE TSOGYAL[49]

The yoga of thatness,
The daily practice of Tsogyal,
From the Six Cycles of Zurza's Tukdam

Padmasambhava and Chokgyur Lingpa
arranged by Karmey Khenpo Rinchen Dargye

Homage to the Guru's Assembly of Dakinis

Among the dakini sadhana cycles of Zurza's Tukdam, *this is the sadhana of innermost* thatness, *the daily practice of Yeshe Tsogyal. It has three parts: preliminaries, main part, and conclusion.*

First, once you have fully received the empowerment for this practice and abide by the samayas, engage in the mind trainings of renunciation and bodhichitta. With enthusiastic vigor, imagine that sentient beings filling all of space take refuge and arouse bodhichitta in the presence of Guru Yeshe Tsogyal, the embodiment of all the objects of refuge, which are in the sky before you. Then repeat each of the following three times:

NAMO:
In the guru, yidam, and dakini,:
The ocean of victorious Three Roots,:
I and all other beings take refuge:
With one-pointed devotion until reaching enlightenment.:

HOH:
All sentient beings have been my mothers.:
In order that they may attain buddhahood,:
I will continuously develop bodhichitta, by refraining from all evil
    deeds,:

---

49 Translated by Erik Pema Kunsang

Practicing virtuous actions, and benefiting others.

May all sentient beings be happy;
May they be free from all suffering;
May they never be apart from joy;
And may they realize the equality of all phenomena.

By repeating this three times, you will train your mind in the four immeasurables. Then say,

HUNG HUNG HUNG

This is the natural sound of the vajra mantra, which expels all maras, obstructors, and perverted guides. Then by saying,

VAJRA GYANA RAKSHA DHRUM

Steadily imagine the protection circle. If you have set out offerings in actuality, consecrate them by saying,

AH HUNG SARVA PUJA MEGHA SAMAYE HUNG

The second has two parts: the primary part of the practice of meditation, which is to visualize the deity, and, as the subsidiary part, entering the samadhi of the recitation. For the first say,

A
Everything is the nonarising dharmadhatu,
Manifesting as the spontaneously present expression of awareness.
The capacity displayed in manifold ways is bam.
E YAM BAM LAM SUM RAM and DHRUM
Become space supporting wind, water, earth,
And Mount Sumeru blazing with flames in the space of the five
   consorts.
Within the protection circle of unchanging vajras,
Amidst the realm of a thousandfold fully bloomed lotus flowers,
Is a celestial palace supported by a vajra cross.
Square in shape and decorated with jewels,
It has four gates, walls, ledges, tiled overhangs,
Lattice designs of lotus flowers and jewels,

Wall colonnades, balustrades, and eight arches,⬧
As well as lotuses, dharma wheels, deer, parasols,⬧
White flowers, and jewel crest ornaments.⬧

In the center of a square jewel,⬧
Upon a multi-colored four-petaled lotus, a sun, and a moon,⬧
Yeshe Tsogyal appears from the letter bam.
Reddish white, she has one face and two arms.⬧
Her right hand, holding a vajra,⬧
Emits a huge cloud of nectar from the thumb and ring finger,⬧
To delight the victorious ones and their sons.⬧
Her left hand, with the gesture of equanimity,⬧
Holds a skull cup filled with nectar.⬧
She wears beautiful silken garments⬧
And is adorned with various jewel ornaments.⬧
Half of her hair is tied up, while the rest flows down freely.⬧
A garland of jewels and flowers graces her hair,⬧
And a crest ornament of gold and turquoise glows with light.⬧
In the posture of a reveling queen, she is seated upon a lotus and
    moon disc.⬧

The four qualified consorts are in the four directions:⬧
The princess holds an arrow with silken streamers and the vase of
    longevity.⬧
Shakya Devi holds up a vajra and bell.⬧
Kalasiddhi raises a khatvanga and a dagger.⬧
Tashi Kyedren brandishes a casket and a dagger.⬧
All are reddish white and the color of their family.⬧
They wear the garments of India, Nepal, and Bhutan.⬧

Four goddesses, bearers of the four mudras,⬧
White, yellow, red, and green, guard the gates.⬧
As our protectors, a gathering of deities and vidyadharas,⬧
Dakinis, dharma protectors, and treasure lords,⬧
Are vividly present like banks of rain clouds.⬧

They are the primordially pure body, speech, and mind,⬧
The nature of the five wisdoms.⬧
OM AH HUNG⬧
OM HUNG TRAM HRIH AH⬧

ABHIKHENTSA HUNG:

Having visualized this, say,

HUNG HRIH:
In the pure realm of dharmadhatu,:
Samantabhadra's consort, engaged in union,:
Has, through the aspiration of boundless compassion,:
Manifested in the form of great enjoyment (sambhogakaya).
Host of dakinis, sporting in magical display,:
With myriad types of pleasing offering articles,:
I invite you with deep faith and yearning.:
All of you, without exception, please come here and join me!:
GYANA CHAKRA VAJRA SAMADZAH:
A HARINISA GYANA DHAKI HRING HRING DZAH DZAH:

By saying,

VAJRA GYANA DZAH HUNG BAM HOH, SAMAYA TISHTHA LHAN,:

Request the invited wisdom beings to remain firmly and indivisibly.
If you would like to make a brief homage and offering, say,

A LA LA HOH, ATIPU HOH, PRATICCHA HOH:

HUNG HRIH:
This offering cloud of Samantabhadra,:
Actually present and mentally created,:
Filling the entire dharmadhatu,:
I offer to Yeshe Tsogyal and her retinue.:
OM ARGHAM PADYAM PUSHPE DHUPE ALOKE GANDHE NAIVIDYA
SHABDA PRATICCHAYE SVAHA:
OM VAJRA RUPA SHABDA RASA SAPARSHE DHARMADHATU
MAHASUKHA PUJA HOH:
SARVA PANCHA AMRITA KHARAM KHAHI:
MAHA RAKTA KHAHI, MAHA BALINGTA KHAHI:
TANA GANA MAHAMUDRA SUKHA DHARMADHATU SVABHAVA
ATMA KO HANG:

Thus offer the outer, inner, secret, and thatness offerings. Then say,

Oм⟐

Glorious unchanging consorts of dharmadhatu,⟐
Enjoying the wealth of great bliss, five supreme families,⟐
Manifold functions, dancers of magical display,⟐
And chief of dakinis, to you I bow down and offer praise!⟐

Boundless activity beyond partiality,⟐
Always timely, free from attachment and obstruction,⟐
Pacifying, increasing, magnetizing, and subjugating;⟐
I praise you who spontaneously fulfill the welfare of beings.⟐

Having praised in this way, focus your attention one-pointedly on the vivid presence of the deities. Arouse firm pride and train in the recollection of pure symbolism.

Second, for training in the recitation visualization, say,

Within the bhandha of space in the heart center,
Rays of light shine forth from the wisdom bam,
Making offerings to all the victorious ones of the ten directions,⟐
And gathering back their blessings in the form of nectar.⟐
The light rays glow, filled with the quintessence of unity.⟐
Overflowing, they pervade my entire body,⟐
Blazing with the wisdom of great bliss.⟐
BAM HARINISA AH⟐

Recite this as the principal mantra. At the end of the session, chant a smaller amount of the following:

BAM HARINISA MAHASUKHA SIDDHI HUNG AH⟐

Third, for the concluding steps, when you are about to rise from the session, amend the duplications and omissions with the mantra of vowels and consonants and stabilize by means of the mantra of the essence of causation. Then say,

OM BENZA ARGHAM PADYAM PUSHPE DHUPE ALOKE GANDHE
NAIVIDYA SHABDA SARVA PANCHA AMRITA RAKTA BALINGTA
MAHAPUJA AH HUNG⟐

Hung§
Bhagavati Vajra Dakini,§
Body, speech, and mind and five wisdoms,§
Fully perfected chief of all dakinis,§
Along with your retinue—to all of you I bow down and offer
  praise.§

*Having made this praise, confess your mistakes with the Hundred Syllable
mantra. Then say,*

Ah§
The pure appearance and existence is absorbed into myself.§
Beyond focus, like a rainbow vanishing into the sky,§
I dissolve into the ultimate deity of luminosity.§
The melody of speech fades away like thunder into space.§
Realized mind is left as dharmadhatu without fabrication.§
A a ah§

Om§
Manifest as the mudras of body, speech, and mind,§
Ah§
My body wears the armor of mantra.§
Hung§
The three mandalas of sights, sounds, and thoughts§
Hoh§
Act indivisibly for the welfare of beings.§
Om ah hung hoh§

Thus emerge in the unified form. Then say,

Hoh§
May this unexcelled accumulation of merit;§
The virtue gathered since beginningless time;§
And the inconceivable, ultimate [merit]§
Be dedicated to the space beyond focus.§

Thus seal with dedication. Then say,

Om§

DAKINI ACTIVITY

The splendor of the empty essence, cognizant nature,§
And the manifestation of the manifold capacity,§
Indivisible, truly enlightened, and unchanging;§
May the goodness of these spontaneously perfect five kayas be
    present!§

*Moreover, utter any other suitable verses of auspiciousness and scatter
flowers.*

This version is extremely condensed for the sake of providing a daily
practice that is easy to apply. When you do a more extensive version,
combine this with the preliminaries, the invitation, offerings, and praises
according to the extensive sadhana and the feast offering according to the
terma root text.

The wisdom dakini Vajravarahi [in person], bearing the name Wang,
who is among the ten holders of this teaching, gave me the command to
write this daily practice belonging to the sadhana cycle of the dakinis,
accompanied by a scarf of auspicious emblems, auspicious divine bro-
cade, gold, and many kashapana coins made of silver. Respectfully vener-
ating her command at the crown of my head, I, Karma Ratna, a khenpo
upholder of the Vinaya and a joyful servant of the great tertön and dharma
king [Chokgyur Lingpa], wrote this at the gandhola of Yamdrog Samdrub
Chöling. May this be a cause for the life of this noble lady vidyadhara to last
for one hundred aeons and for all the infinite sentient beings to realize the
wisdom body of the immortal Mandarava Vajrayogini.

SARVA MANGALAM

THE VAJRA BRIDGE[50]

An Aspiration for the Gradual Path
of the Celestial Dakinis[51]

Chokgyur Lingpa

Lama yeshe khandro gongsu sol
Garzhuk ogmin nechog dampa ney
Kalden daggi düngyi namkhar la
Ngönsum shekney gyepey denla zhuk

Wisdom dakini guru, listen to me!
Please appear in person from wherever you dwell
In the sublime and eminent abode of Akanishtha,
And settle on this splendid throne in the sky before this worthy
   person!

Lü-ngag yisum güpey chaktsal zhing
Chinang sangwa dezhin nyikyi chö
Damtsig nyamchag galtrül tamchey shak
Sangngak chöpa namla jeyi rang
Mindröl zabmöi chökhor korwar kül
Nyangen mida kalgyar zhukpar sol

With respectful body, speech, and mind, I bow down
And present you with outer, inner, secret, and thatness offerings.
I apologize for every breach of samaya, every offence and mistake,
And rejoice in everyone practicing the Secret Mantra.
I implore you to turn the profound Dharma Wheel of ripening and
   liberation.
Do not pass into nirvana but remain for a hundred aeons.

---

50 Translated by Erik Pema Kunsang
51 *mkha' spyod mkha' 'gro'i lam rim gyi smon lam rdo rje'i zam pa bzhugs so*

Düsum sakdang yöpey gewa nam
Küntu zangpöi chötrin chenpor gyur
Lama gyalwa seydang cheyla bül
Khakyab phamar gyurpey drola ngo

All the virtue I possess and gather throughout the three times,
Has become an immense offering cloud of Samantabhadra.
I offer it to the guru, the victorious ones and their sons,
And dedicate this to all beings, my parents filling [all of] space!

Khorwey dungel malü zhiwar shog
Detar sangye dzeypar rabdrub pey
Sönam taye dampa gangtob chi
Dagzhen namkyi gyüla nyurdu min

May all the sufferings of samsara subside!
May all this sublime and boundless merit,
Whatever is achieved from fulfilling the deeds of the buddhas,
Quickly ripen in my mind and the minds of others!

Daljor phünsum tsokpey lüten di
Tobpar kala jigpar lawa dang
Gyumdrey lumey sipey dukha sok
Tsülzhin shepey ngejung gikül wey
Khamdrug denpey dönden jepar shog

Inspired by the renunciation gained by correctly understanding
That this body, with perfect freedoms and riches,
Is hard to obtain and perishes easily,
That cause and effect are unfailing, and that samsaric existence is
    suffering,
May I use to advantage this support endowed with the six elements!

Lama könchog sumla lokhel zhing
Semchen phamar shepey nyingje yi
Nyechö kündom gewey chöla tsön
Sampa zangpöi zhenphen tagtu gyi

By entrusting myself to the guru and the Three Jewels
And engaging compassion that acknowledges all beings as my
    parents,

May I refrain from all evil deeds, endeavor in what is virtuous,
And, with noble intention, always act for the benefit of others!

Gewey shenyen namkyi jesu zung
Tösam gompey rangyü lekpar dröl
Lama dampey kadrin sumgyi kyang
Kusung tukyi damla neypar shog

May all the spiritual teachers accept me,
And may learning, reflection, and meditation fully liberate my
    being.
May the sublime master foster me with his threefold kindness,
And may I abide by the samayas of body, speech, and mind!

Khyepar küntu zangpo yabdang yum
Dorje sempa yeshe khandro ma
Pema benza tsogyal manda ra
Chokgyur dechen lingpa dechen yum
Gyüpey lama namkyi mangag di
Tsülzhin nyamsu langwey jinlab kyi
Nyamdang tokpey drötsey nyurdu min
Lamey namtar trinley drubpar shog

In particular, may I correctly practice the instructions of all these
    lineage gurus:
Samantabhadra, the father with consort,
Vajrasattva and the wisdom dakini,
Padma Vajra, Tsogyal, and Mandarava,
Chokgyur Dechen Lingpa and his consort Dechen.
By the blessings of doing so, may signs of experience and
    realization quickly ripen,
And may I emulate the guru's example and fulfill his activities!

Chidrub drölmey barchey künsel zhing
Lhaküi tengyi wangpo tseydu pheb
Yila gompey lharnang walgyi shar
Tsenmey yülsum mimik ngangzhag pey
Jinggö jyurbüi kyöndang nampar drel

Through the outer sadhana of Tara, may I dispel all obstacles
And reach full capacity through the bodily form of the deity.

By cultivating it in my mind, may the deity's presence manifest
   vividly,
And by resting in the nonconceptual state without the focus of the
   three objects,
May I be totally free from the defects of dullness, agitation, and
   rigidity!

Kyerim nyamnga rimpar dzogpar yi
Kudog lasok wangpöi yüldu sal
Zhenpey yülkün lhakur dagpar shog

By gradually perfecting the five experiences of the development
   stage,
May I perceive the color of the body and so forth, manifest as
   objects of the senses,
And may all apprehended objects be purified into deity!

Nangdrub naljor mayi tünkyen dzom
Tsayi düdröl lükyi trülgyur nü
Lungla wangtob ngagi denpa drub
Tigle dechen gosum shintu jang

Through the inner sadhana of [Vajra] yogini, may favorable
   conditions assemble,
May the nadi-knots be untied, and may I possess the power to
   conjure and project emanations of my body!
May I gain mastery over prana and achieve the truthfulness of
   speech,
And may the bindus be refined into the three doors of great bliss!

Sangdrub sangwa yeshe phonye lam
Pemey yumchey gosum jinlab pey
Dagpey dushe sumden gawa zhi
Tigle ronyam dechen tokpar shog

Through the secret sadhana, the phonya path of Secret Wisdom,
May I consecrate the three doors and the lotus consort.
By possessing the threefold pure notions,
May I realize [the] great bliss, the same taste of the bindus of the
   four joys!

Yangsang manda rawey chimey lam
Khordey chülön zeykyi zhenpa drel
Tummo rabbar gangtrö neyül nyul
Nyemje nyamnga mepey tülzhuk kyi
Düzhi pungchom chimey tsensa zin
Riwo tse-nga pota layi ney
Ngayab orgyen yüldang shambha la
Neyül tsok kyi duwar chöpar shog

Through the innermost path, the immortality of Mandarava,
May I be free from attachment to food, by extracting the essences of
  samsara and nirvana!
By setting the tummo ablaze, may I roam the snow mountains, the
  sacred lands and places!
With the yogic conduct of transcending fear and indecision,
May I defeat the armies of the four maras and capture the
  stronghold of immortality!
On the Five-Peaked Mountain and [at] the Potala,
On Chamara, in Uddiyana, and in Shambhala,
May I partake in the feast gatherings of the sacred lands and places!

Dekho nanyi yeshe tsogyal gyi
Sherab zabmöi dagdzin chingwa dröl
Gompey rangsem tongpa nyidu ney
Dela dzinpa drelwey lhagtong tok

Through the thatness sadhana of Yeshe Tsogyal,
May deep knowledge undo the bond of ego-clinging,
May meditation allow my mind to remain in emptiness,
And may I realize the insight free from fixation on it!

Machö rangtog nyidu rang-ngo trö
Chökün deyi tsaldu tagchö pey
Tsidab meypar rangdröl dingtob ney
Namtog trekchö tawa tokpar shog

Without fabrication, may I recognize my natural face, in itself,
And resolve that all phenomena are the expression of this nature!
Gaining confidence in my mind, free from appraising,
May I realize the view of cutting through conceptual thinking!

Döney rangla nepey yeshe kham
Özer ngaden tiglei tsülshar wa
Yöpa mayin ngöpo chirma drub
Meypa mayin wangpöi ngönsum tong

The wisdom nature, which is primordially present within me,
Appears as bindus endowed with five-colored rays of light.
They don't exist, since they have no solidity whatsoever.
They don't not exist, since they appear before my very eyes.

Zungwey yülmin rangi rigpey dang
Dzinpey semmin togmey ngangdu char
Redok machö ngangdu zhagpey tse
Yeshe nangwa lammer charwar shog

They are not perceived objects but the radiance of my own awareness.
They are the perceiving mind as they manifest in the state of
    nonconception.
When I rest in the state untouched by hope and fear,
May the manifestations of wisdom appear bright and vivid!

Makö tsombu dagpey nangwa de
Yigdru chagtsen nyamnang gongdu chey
Kudang yeshe rigpa tseydu pheb
Zungdzin lozey döchey chönam zey

These pure visions of unmade clusters
Increase as syllables, attributes, and so forth.
The kayas and wisdoms of rigpa reach fullness,
The concepts of perceiver and perceived vanish, and material
    phenomena are exhausted.

Zhönnu bumku chöku ngönsum tok
Longchö dzokpey zhingdu ngönsang gye
Trülpey zhingdu möpa natsok la
Gangdül dertön drodön lhündrub shog

When directly realizing the dharmakaya of the youthful vase,
May I attain true enlightenment in the realm of sambhogakaya!
In the realms of nirmanakaya, in accordance with the various
    inclinations,

May I spontaneously perfect the welfare of beings, by appearing in whatever way is beneficial!

Zhenyang phomey jalü dorjei ku
Pema jungney bima mitra zhin
Trinley zhiyi drowa küntül ney
Ngagkyi tenpa yünring dzinpar shog

Moreover, in the unchanging and indestructible form of the rainbow body,
Just like Padmakara and Vimalamitra,
May I influence beings through the four activities
And uphold the teachings of Mantra for a long time!

Tsedir sangye kawa meypa drub
Logyar tsozhing neymey langtso den
Tünkyen rabjor gosum chöla chö
Tendang drowey phendey drubpar shog

In this life, may I attain buddhahood without hardship
And may I live for a hundred years, youthful and in good health!
May I possess favorable conditions; apply my body, speech, and mind to the Dharma;
And accomplish the welfare of the teachings and beings!

Khachö ngagkyi drubpey damdzey kyi
Trelwar tigle jepey mangag chey
Zhingkye duwey drongdu kyöpey tse
Neynyül khandro mintsam gakyil chen

Through the instruction of smearing a spot on my forehead
With the samaya substance consecrated by the dakini mantra,
When I journey through the citadels where terrestrial dakinis gather,
May I meet a dakini with the coil-of-joy between her brows on her way to the sacred places!

Treyma tagtu dayi lentrö de
Daggi lagpey trikma neyzung te
Yeshe khandröi zhingdu triney kyang
Naljor mayi jesu zungwar shog

As soon as we meet and I understand the symbolic sign,
May she take me by the hand and
Lead me to the realm of the wisdom dakinis,
And may the yoginis there accept me!

Galtey tsedi phenpa zepey tse
Shi-ngen gumpa chobgye mijung zhing
Neychö zugngu drakpöi mitse war
Khorwa lodog zhenpa kündrel shog

In any case, if it happens that the force of this life runs out,
May the eighteen sadistic killers with evil disposition not appear.
Unharmed by the intense pain when my life force interrupts,
May I be totally free from attachment and turn away from samsara!

Gewa cheche digpa chungchung ngu
Sangye zhenney mitsöl lasok pey
Daka yeshe lola rabngey ney
Deney dedror trowa kyewar shog

With the greatest virtue and the slightest misdeeds,
Without seeking buddhahood elsewhere, and so forth,
May I clearly sustain the "wisdom of passing" in my mind
And may I possess the joy of proceeding to ever-greater happiness!

Mögü nyingje tsemey kyidrang wey
Redok kündrel mayeng tingdzin den
Trülnang tamchey gyuma tartok pey
Jungwa ngatim dugsum togpa gak

Inspired by immeasurable devotion and compassion,
May I possess unwavering samadhi, free from all hope and fear!
When I realize that all deluded experiences are like magical
    illusions,
May the thoughts of the three poisons cease upon the dissolving of
    the five elements!

Nangchey tobsum ösel latim tsey
Rang-ngo tröney chökur ngönsang gye
Deley dangtse ö-nga zhitröi ku
Ngöngom ngoshey longku drubpar shog

When the appearance, increase, and attainment dissolve into
    luminosity,
May I recognize my natural face and truly awaken into
    dharmakaya!
Upon emerging from that, may I accomplish sambhogakaya
    through the familiarity of former training,
By recognizing the five-colored light and the forms of the peaceful
    and wrathful deities!

Marig wanggi deley yelgyur na
Tsawey lama rigdzin gyamtsöi tsok
Sangwey yumchog yeshe khandro ma
Ngönsum daggi dündu jönpar shog

If, by the power of ignorance, I waver from that state,
May the root guru and the ocean-like gathering of vidyadharas,
The wisdom dakinis, and the supreme secret consorts,
Appear in actuality before me!

Khachö neysu droshe sungtö ney
Sangye ngönsum tongwey deymö kye
Dukdang gyaltsen baden rölmor chey
Daki neysu taler tripar shog

Upon hearing their voices saying, "Come to the celestial realms!",
May I feel the devotion of meeting the Buddha in person!
With parasols and banners, streamers and music,
May they lead me directly to the realm of the dakinis!

Yingchuk khandröi phodrang goru chin
Yeshe kyilkhor deru zhukma tag
Nyönmong dribpa malü derjang ney
Dorje phagmöi zhelchog tongwar shog

When reaching the gate of the palace of the dakini Queen of Space,
May I immediately enter the wisdom mandala!
May all the obscurations of disturbing emotions be purified right
    there,
And may I behold the eminent face of Vajravarahi!

Künzang chöpey tringyi nyejey ney
Sumpey wangkur lungten dampa tob
Uk-yung sachu tobney ngönsang gye
Trülpa dumey drodön jepar shog

Pleasing her with cloud banks of Samantabhadra offerings,
May I receive the third empowerment, the prophecy, and the
    precepts!
May I gain reassurance, attain the ten bhumis, reach true
    enlightenment,
And act for the welfare of beings through myriad emanations!

Leydang kyengyi khorwar kyamna yang
Kyewa küntu lamar midrel zhing
Kusung tukchog nyepey phüldu gyur
Dagpey khorgyi togmar kyewar shog

Even if I do stray into samsara due to karma and misfortune,
May I never part from the guru in any of my lives!
May I offer the finest service to his body, speech, and mind
And always be born among the first of his pure retinue!

Palden lama namkyi jinlab dang
Sangye jangsem namkyi tukje gang
Daggi lhagsam nampar dagpa yi
Mönlam jitab zhindu nyurdrub shog

By the blessings of all the glorious gurus,
By the compassion of all the buddhas and bodhisattvas,
And by the purity of my noble intentions,
May these aspirations be quickly fulfilled in accordance with my
    wishes!

Venerable Lama Ngedön whose mind is utterly liberated through the
profound teachings, offered me a divine raiment and a crystal rosary with
one hundred and eight beads and made the request to write an aspiration
such as this. In response, I, Chokgyur Dechen Lingpa, composed this in
Glorious Lhasa, the site where dakinis assemble, on the tenth day of the
waxing moon. It was written down by Rinchen Namgyal, an expounder
of the five sciences. Sarva mangalam!

APPENDIX I[52]

Dakini Script

Orgyen Tobgyal Rinpoche

In the *Lamrim Yeshe Nyingpo*, the second main heading is called "Explaining the Sign Script and the Homage," which is the reason for the sign script, and the meaning of paying homage. Here's a quote from *the Tantra of Secrets*:

> Dakinis make use of symbols.
> They are skilled in symbols and symbolic replies.
> They link the ultimate essence to symbolism.
> Dakinis are the life force of symbols.

The dakini script that makes use of symbols is impossible to decipher by anyone other than a person who is of equal status to the dakinis. And, since most of the profound teachings existing as terma treasures are encoded in symbolic script, and therefore originate from the secret treasury of the dakinis, they do not lie within the reach of experience of the ordinary learned or accomplished masters of India and Tibet.

This means the person has to have an extraordinary special mandate, a transmission directly from Padmasambhava, in order to understand what is within the dakini script. No one else can do that, no matter how learned. If you show the dakini script to Tsongkhapa Lobsang Drakpa, or to Sakya Pandita, or to the Indian great panditas, like Jnanakirti, they probably wouldn't understand. But also the dakini script differs from tertön to tertön. You have to have the specific mandate for that. Unless you have the karmic destiny to reveal that, you won't be able to decode it. Thus, one tertön won't necessarily be able to decipher another tertön's dakini script.

While I was in Bir, one woman from America came there and said she wanted to meet me. When I came to the door, she said, "I want to learn dakini script. I heard you have some of these. I want to see them and learn how to read them, and I want to learn dakini writing. Are you going to teach me?" I replied, "There is no way you can study and learn dakini writing." She had already asked the Dalai Lama. And he had told her, "If you are a tertön, then maybe there is some chance, but otherwise not at all." Then the woman said, "You are the son in the family line of a tertön, so maybe you know something."

Then I said, "If you want to learn it, you should learn it from a tertön directly. Still, there may be a way that is even easier than going to a tertön: Chant the aspiration for rebirth in the Copper-Colored Mountain buddhafield one hundred thousand times. Then, when you're reborn in Guru Rinpoche's pure land, you can ask him directly. Guru Padmasambhava is the only one who knows all the different kinds of symbolic script; probably nobody else does." Then she asked, "Is there no other way?" Then I replied. "No!" Then she said, "Don't you have some of the yellow parchment?" And I said, "Yes, I do." And she said, "Please show me. I want to see it." And then I said, "No, I won't show you." She said, "I also have some." Then, I said, "If you already have some, that should be enough, shouldn't it." Then she put her hand down in her bag and took up one book by Tulku Thondup. There is some dakini script printed in there, and she showed me that. And actually, she could partially read it. Then I said, "That's amazing! If you can read dakini script, maybe you should reveal some termas as well. However, I'm not going to show you any of the dakini script that I have."

It is only the tertön who can really comprehend the meaning of the dakini script. It's a quote here:

> Treasure letters are the body of magical creation.
> They are also speech to understand sounds and words.[53]

Actually, the symbolic writing is a form of the nirmanakaya, and when a person has the right karmic destiny, he or she will, by means of a profound coincidence of place, time, and aspiration, be able to decode it. So, these letters are born in the nirmanakaya, and from them, even if there are only seven, many volumes of scriptures can be written down, because the tertön is able to hear the sound and comprehend the meaning. They are also speech.

On the shrine in the Rigpa Center in San Francisco, in front of Guru Rinpoche's statue, there is a photo of a dakini script that comes from Chokgyur Lingpa, from the cycle called Sampa Lhündrub. I was astonished to see it there on the shrine. It has seven characters, and when Chokgyur Lingpa looked at the seventh one, he said it was an inexhaustible city of dakini script. When Dilgo Khyentse looked at it, he would sometimes be able to reveal inexhaustible mind treasures. The real piece is in Sikkim. So, if you have the chance once, maybe you can go and see it, and maybe you can reveal some termas. It is quite risky to see a terma sign, which is inexhaustible.

As I mentioned earlier, the person endowed with the karmic continuation will be able to decode the symbolic meaning of these nirmanakaya treasure letters, the vajra forms endowed with all eminent aspects, and establish them correctly in writing. To indicate this, seven symbolic letters have been placed at the beginning of this book.

There are three reasons for putting dakini script at the beginning of a text: First, these treasure letters are the seal of command of the Second Buddha, the Master of Uddiyana. His seal is directly represented by symbolic signs, indicating that the transmission has not been corrupted by ordinary people; thus, the source is authentic. It's the same as when a king's decree has his seal at the bottom, showing that it is a bona fide word of the king to be heeded. In the same way, the terma signs at the beginning of a scripture show that it is the authentic speech of Padmasambhava.

The second reason relates to the teaching, which translates the secret code of the dakinis, without altering the symbols, mistaking the words, or confusing the meaning. This indicates that the profound instruction and great blessing of the original scripture remain potent and unblemished, as the terma text has not been altered, mistaken, or confused in any way. Who can actually witness that? Jamyang Khyentse Wangpo, the most important of the five tertön kings, witnessed that. Among all one hundred and eight major tertöns that appeared in Tibet, the two later ones, Jamyang Khyentse and Chokgyur Lingpa, both possessed what is called the "seven transmissions." In the past, no one was said to have these seven transmissions.

The first of these seven is the oral tradition of Kama, which both of these masters received. This is a transmission mandate originating from

Padmasambhava and Vimalamitra. It has been passed down through empowerment, reading transmission, explanation of tantras, and the authorization to be "indivisible from me." Therefore, this first one is called the "four rivers of transmission" given by Padmasambhava and Vimalamitra. Together, they form the first transmission, called the "oral tradition of Kama." The second is the earth treasure revelation, such as Lama Tennyi Korsum, and many other earth treasures. At one point, Jamyang Khyentse Wangpo saw in a pure vision that the entire land of Tibet had buried treasures, terma teachings, everywhere. He saw all of them clearly, as though placed in the palm of his own hand. Concerning many of the termas that Chokgyur Lingpa revealed, Jamyang Khyentse first received the "address" of where they were located, and then he sent Chokgyur Lingpa out to fetch them. Jamyang Khyentse didn't always write down the addresses, which sometimes came on little scrolls, as they were simply too secret, and he was afraid that some tertön thief would reveal them at the wrong time. For example, Yeshe Tsogyal immediately wrote down the Dzogchen Desum, the Three Sections of the Great Perfection, and handed it to Jamyang Khyentse Wangpo, putting it exactly in the rice bowl in front of him.

Some tertöns only reveal articles, ritual articles, and the like, or precious substances. Some only reveal teachings and no material things. Jamyang Khyentse and Chokgyur Lingpa, however, revealed both teachings and articles, as if taking them out from a huge treasury. Jamgön Kongtrül once sent a letter to Jamyang Khyentse, saying, "I need a little statue to put in the heart center of Dorje Sempa, a huge Vajrasattva statue that I'm building. Can you please give me a really special one?" Then Jamyang Khyentse invoked the dharma protector Dorje Yudrönma, and she went to a place in India called Palri, the site of the stupa remains of King Jah, one of the great kings of India. She brought a small Vajrasattva statue from there, and placed it right on his desk, instantaneously. So, these two masters also had power over earth treasures.

They also had what is called yangter, rediscovered treasures. For example, Jamyang Khyentse revealed Tsasum Drildrub, which had been discovered in the past; he rediscovered it. He also had mind treasures, such as the Chime Pagma Nyingtig. Furthermore, he had many types of transmissions, such as Purpa and Yangdak, that belong to the hearing lineage. Jamyang Khyentse also had the transmission of pure vision.

For instance, after Chokgyur Lingpa passed away, he manifested in the sambhogakaya pure land where Chokgyur Lingpa took the form of the buddha called Pema Nyugu. Jamyang Khyentse wrote down a teaching called Kusum Rikdü Zabtig, which is based on that pure vision.

In addition, he had what is called "recollection of a former life," wherein he had total recall of being tertön Chökyi Wangchük,[54] [one of the five tertön kings] and, thus, he revealed the Chetsün Nyingtig, the heart essence of that great tertön. This happened when Jamyang Khyentse was near Chimphu, in the upper part of a valley in Reding. All the phenomena of this world dissolved, and he had a recollection of his past life as Chetsün Senge Wangchuk and revealed Chetsün Nyingtig, the Heart Essence of the Great Chetsün, which is like the quintessence of all the Dzogchen teachings.

Since these two masters possessed the great seven transmissions, and they were both there, looking at each other, when this text [Lamrim Yeshe Nyingpo] was revealed, I feel confident that it is free from mistakes and confusion. Such a teaching has great blessing.

The third reason to place the sign script at the beginning pertains to potential recipients. Just as someone born blind cannot adequately examine an elephant, people lacking the right fortune cannot even partially comprehend the symbolic script, no matter how sharp-minded they may be. You can therefore trust that the treasure master transcends the scope of common people.

Someone like me wouldn't even see one single syllable to write down, even if I soaked the dakini script in water for a hundred days and stared at it. The way to decode yellow parchment with dakini script is to soak it in water mixed with the five nectars and perform a ganachakra, a feast offering. Miraculously, the writing will then start to appear. The paper doesn't sink in the water; it doesn't dissolve either, but the script will start to appear.

Even though I am not a tertön, myself, I know about tertöns. You don't have to write the revelation down immediately once the magical writing manifests. As a matter of fact, it is better not to write it down immediately. It's much better to supplicate one-pointedly to Padmasambhava and mingle your minds together so that they are indivisible. And then, within that state of samadhi, whatever manifests will be exactly the appropriate amount and meaning to influence people. Then you write that down correctly. Once it is recorded on paper, the previous script vanishes, and the next will appear. This is not within the reach of normal people, right? No one can make that up. It is something to trust in; it's trustworthy. That was an explanation of the reason why the *Lamrim Yeshe Nyingpo* [and other treasure texts] begin with some sign script.

APPENDIX II[55]

Jamgön Kongtrül

Explaining the Instruction on the Four Stakes[56] to Bind the Life Force

This has four points: The stake of concentration [samadhi], the stake of the essence mantra, the stake of the activity of emanation and absorption, and the stake of unchanging realization.[57]

THE STAKE OF CONCENTRATION

This has two points: training in the power of concentration, and the measure of the training together with its result.

Training in the Power of Concentration

The *Lamrim Yeshe Nyingpo* root text says,

> In all cases, fix your mind in one-pointed concentration.
> Since you are perfecting the mind as the form of the deity,
> Arrange a [deity] form, such as a gross or subtle image,
> Placing it skillfully as a support for visualization.
> Straighten your body, expel the stale breath, and focus your mind, eyes, and breath one-pointedly.
> Meditate in short sessions, repeatedly.
> As your practice develops, prolong the sessions, in order to fully train in the progressive steps
> Of movement, attainment, familiarity, and steadiness, until you achieve perfection.
>
> Clear away all shortcomings in samadhi, such as dullness, agitation, and so forth.

---

56 Also translated as nails.

At times, relax into the innate state of nonthought.⁑

Sometimes practice while developing proficiency in the form of the
   deity.⁑

Look into the nature, in which the deity is indivisible from your
   mind.⁑

Use all experience as the display of wisdom.⁑

No matter which of these visualization methods you employ, in all
cases, it is essential to possess the instructions on the "four stakes to bind
the life force." In this way, you will be able to firmly realize that the body,
speech, and mind of the peaceful and wrathful sugatas and your own
three gates are the great state of equal taste. The Tantra of Secret Perfection describes this, stating,

> In any case, whether wisdom or mundane,
> Unless you plant the four stakes to bind the life force,
> It is always unfruitful, like a barren woman.
> The means to completely capture the life force of the Glorious One
> Is to know one, and thereby attain all life forces.
> For example, when Rahu's mouth
> Eats the single sun in the sky,
> He captures the thousandfold life force of
> All the suns, [reflected] in a thousand ponds, without even trying.
> This is why the four stakes that bind the life force are crucial.

In accordance with this statement, as a beginner you should focus
your attention with one-pointed concentration on the form of the deity's
body, without letting it move elsewhere. You should plant the stake of
samadhi, since you are perfecting the mind, with its eight collections of
consciousness, as the kaya-forms and wisdoms of the deity. It is phrased
in this way,

> For the stake of samadhi, fix your attention one-pointedly
> On the kapala form, and do not wander.

As just mentioned, to begin, arrange the deity's single mudra form.
For the subtle aspect, set out a clearly painted seed syllable, such as a
white ah or a blue hung the size of a cubit. For the gross aspect, you can

use an authentic image of the deity painted on a kapala.[58] Place it before you as a visualization support, making sure it is level and close by, as a practitioner skilled in the ways of development [stage] would do.

Having done this, sit on a comfortable seat, straighten your body, and expel the stale breath three times. Focus one-pointedly on the visualization support—integrating your mind's attention, the gaze of your eyes, and the coming and going of your breath—without letting these three factors be separated. Train repeatedly for short periods. Through this, you will gradually undergo the following five experiences.[59]

When your attention does not remain on the visualization support, but, rather, moves restlessly with numerous thought formations, that is the experience of movement, which is like a waterfall. Following that, thoughts subside to some extent, and your attention remains for the most part on the visualization support. When you become strongly habituated to the mental expression of that image, and the visualization appears vividly in your mind, even when your eyes are closed, that is the experience of attainment, which is like a river flowing in a gorge.

When you are able to bring the visualization support to mind, vividly and exactly, as you are training in it, and you can change its size and appearance in various ways at will without thoughts straying away from it, that is the experience of familiarity, which is like the gentle flow of a great river. By training in mingling the deity's form and your mind indivisibly, when your attention can remain for as long as you wish on the entire bodily form without being interrupted by any thought whatsoever, that is the experience of immovability [steadiness], which is like a pond undulating from a breeze. When, in addition to this, you are able to visualize down to the details of the white and black of the eyes and the pores of the body hair, and the eight measures of clarity and steadiness have reached full strength, without [your attention] being captured by any object or situation at any time day or night, that is the experience of perfection, which is like the great ocean free from waves.

Until this has happened, in order to become fully trained and not grow weary in the beginning, you should gradually prolong the duration of the practice sessions, as you become more and more proficient.

As you train, various shortcomings may arise: dullness, which is a lack of mental clarity; agitation, which is a restless movement; and others, such as drowsiness, torpor, and scatteredness. When any of these shortcomings occur within your samadhi, you should recognize them and, without straying into indifference, clear them all away by applying their respective antidotes.[60]

The methods for developing and bringing forth enhancement in this have been taught within Nyang Ral Nyima Özer's terma called Replies to Questions from Yeshe Tsogyal, in the Lama Gongdü, and elsewhere. Their key points can be summarized under six headings, such as deity training and so forth.[61]

At times, take rest, while naturally relaxing your thinking mind into the innate state of nonthought.

Sometimes train in visualizing the form of the deity in various ways. Modulate the size, picturing it as huge as Mount Sumeru and as tiny as a mustard seed. Apply different colors and shapes. Imagine the deity in different situations of daily life, both close and distant, and in various places.[62] Train in this way until you develop proficiency.

Sometimes look into the nature of the real condition by means of mingling indivisibly the deity's form and your mind.[63] Abandon the dualistic fixation of meditation object and act of meditating, while recognizing the natural face of the meditator; through this, sustain the yoga of the meditation state.

In post-meditation, consider all sights, sounds, and thoughts as the uninterrupted state of original wakefulness. Regard what you wear as the peaceful and wrathful attire, food and drink as ganachakra, walking and sitting as vajra dance, and so forth. In short, make use of all experiences, no matter what you encounter, as being exclusively the display of the wisdom deity.[64]

TIBETAN SOURCE MATERIAL

Chokling Tersar BA: Author: Chokgyur Lingpa, (*mchog gyur gling pa*)

zab bdun rtsa gsum tshe'i zab pa las padma mkha' 'gro'i phrin las sngon 'gro khyer bde ldeb 265–269

Kurukulle Preliminaries

zab bdun rtsa gsum tshe'i zab pa las dbang gi las sbyor padma mka' 'gro'i sgrub thabs 271–276

The Sadhana of the Lotus Dakini for Magnetizing

zab bdun padma mkha' 'gro'i gud byang dbang gi thig le gnad byang tshig brgyud ma bcas ldeb 293–296

The Essence of Magnetizing

zab bdun rtsa gsum tshe'i zab pa las padma mkha' 'gro'i tshog mchod sogs rjes kyi las rim snying por dril ba mkha' 'gro dgyes pa'i rol mo ldeb 297–305

Music to Delight the Dakinis

lha chen dbang phyug yab yum las la bskul ba ldeb 359–361

Invoking the Activity of Lord Mahadeva and Consort

Exact Sources not found, Author: Jamyang Khyentse Wangpo

Short Tsok Offering of the Powerful Lady Kurukulle—Written by Jamyang Khyentse Wangpo

Pema Tseyi Nyingtig—Revealed by Jamyang Khyentse Wangpo.

The Instruction of the Dakinis of Immortality, from *Pema Tseyi Nyingtig, The Heart Essence of Lotus Life*

Chokling Tersar GA: Author: Chokgyur Lingpa, (*mchog gyur gling pa*)

Extracted from *Lamey Tukdrub Barchey Kunsel,* (*phrin las rgyas pa*).

Four Activities, from Dispeller of Obstacles

Chokling Tersar KA: Author: Chokgyur Lingpa, (*mchog gyur gling pa*)

Thugs sgrub zhal gdams snying byang las, lus kyi mchod sbyin bzhugs According to *Tukdrub Sheldam Nyingjang*, the Heart Essence Practice Manual of Oral Instructions.

The Offering and Giving of the Body

Chokling Tersar WA: Chokgyur Lingpa, (*mchog gyur gling pa*)

gdams zab be bum mkha' 'gro gsang ba ye shes kyi brgyud 'debs bde chen sprin phung ldeb 343–344

The Supplication to the Lineage of the Dakini

gdams zab be bum kyi dmar byang mkha' 'gro gsang ba ye shes kyi phrin las
  'dod pa kun 'grub dbang dang las tshogs bcas ldeb 345–374
The Sadhana of the Dakini Sangwa Yeshe

Chokling Tersar LA: Chokgyur Lingpa, (*mchog gyur gling pa*)
brgyud pa'i bla ma rnams la gsol ba 'debs pa byin rlabs sprin dpung bzhugs so
Cloud Banks of Blessings
zur bza'i thugs dam skor drug las de kho na nyid mtsho rgyal gyi nyams len
  rgyun gyi rnal 'byor ldeb 177–183
The Daily Practice of Yeshe Tsogyal

mkha' spyod mkha' 'gro'i lam rim gyi smon lam rdo rje'i zam pa bzhugs
  193–200
The Vajra Bridge

NOTES

1　This was gradually decoded from the yellow parchment as the *Dzogchen Desum,* which the incarnated great tertön Chokgyur Lingpa revealed from the ceiling of the Lotus Crystal Cave, and Khyentse Wangpo, the joyful servant of the Lotus-Born Guru, put into writing. May it be virtuous. Extracted from Jamgön Kongtrül Rinpoche's colophon of the history of *The Sections of the Great Perfection,* entitled, *The Heart Tika History.*

2　Tulku Urgyen Rinpoche, *Blazing Splendor,* trans. and eds. Erik Pema Kunsang and Marcia Binder Schmidt (Hong Kong: Rangjung Yeshe Publications, 2005). Dilgo Khyentse Rinpoche, *Brilliant Moon,* trans. and ed. Ani Jinba Palmo (Boston: Shambhala Publications, Inc, 2009), 280, 284.

3　At this point, one can include the supplications to Guru Rinpoche as well as the general lineage prayers: *Tsigdun Soldeb, Kusum Soldeb, Choku Kunsang, Kunsang Dorsem, Damdzin Namtrul,* and *Ogmin Chokyi,* all of which are found in the extensive version of *Trinley Nyingpo.*

4　Prior to chanting the refuge and bodhichitta, you can include *the Sangchoe Jinlab (short),* or *the Jinlab Namnga* and *Kartor* (extensive).

5　Ocean of Amrita

6　The consecration of the gektor can be included here.

7　The pronunciation of the full mantra is: OM SOBHAVA SHUDDHO SARVA DHARMA SOBHAVA SHUDDHO A HANG

8　The terton name of Jamgön Kongtrül the First.

9　If the refuge and bodhichitta have already been chanted, then it is not necessary to repeat here.

10　At this point, the praise from the *Additional Manual* can be added in as a substitute for the following four lines of praise.

11　The base is both the buddhafield and the celestial palace.

12　When making feast offering, it is not necessary to chant this mantra.

13　Translated by Eric Pema Kungsang

14　Karmey Khenpo Rinchen Dargye.

15　Repeat the traditional four lines and the consecration mantra.

16　Conclude with *Chokchu Dushi* and other dedications, aspirations, verses of auspiciousness, and so forth, as in the extensive version of *Tukdrub Trinley Nyingpo.*

17　Translated by Eric Pema Kungsang

18　OM MAHADEVA DZA Ḥ UMA DEVI HRING HARINISA SIDDHI DZA Ḥ

19　Translated by Eric Pema Kungsang & Marcia B. Schmidt

20　The seven preliminary sections are: 1. The Lineage Supplication, 2. The Terma Root Text for Refuge and bodhicitta, 3. Commanding the obstructing spirits, 4. Drawing the Boundary for Protection, 5. The Gesture of Homage, Confession of Faults, and Taking the Oath, 6. Bringing down the Great Resplendence of Wisdom, 7. Terma Root Text for Consecrating the Offerings.

21 Padmasambhava and Jamgön Kongtrül, *Light of Wisdom,* Volume 1, trans. Erik Pema Kunsang, (Hong Kong: Rangjung Yeshe Publications, 1999), 253.The seven transmissions are: (1) Kama, the Oral Transmission, the early translated Tripitaka and tantras passed on uninterruptedly from master to disciple; (2) Earth Treasure, revealed by the terton; (3) Rediscovered Treasure, revealed for the second time from a past treasure; (4) Mind Treasure, revealed from the mind of the guru; (5) Hearing Lineage, received directly from an enlightened being; (6) Pure Vision, received in a pure experience; and (7) Recollection, remembrance from a former life.

22 For an extensive explanation of fire offering, see Padmasambhava and Jamgön Kongtrül, *Light of Wisdom, The Conclusion,* trans. Erik Pema Kunsang, (Hong Kong: Rangjung Yeshe Publications, 2013), 18–25.

23 Translated by Gyurme Avertin & Marcia B. Schmidt

24 This teaching comes from a commentary on Padma Khandro by Rongdzom Mahapandita in the Rinchen Terdzod.

25 See Appendix II

26 Translated by Lama Chönam & Sangye Khandro

27 Translated by Han Kop

28 From the termas of Chokgyur Lingpa

29 Translated by Erik Pema Kunsang

30 The progressive order of the twelve links of dependent origination. The reverse order is their opposite.

31 The world, the vajra body, and the state of mind.

32 Her Sanskrit name is Padma Dhatvishvari.

33 King, subject, and companion are King Trisong Deütsen, the great Lotsawa Vairochana, and the Dakini Yeshe Tsogyal.

34 Padma Do-ngak Lingpa Ösel Trülpey Dorje is the special tertön name of Jamyang Khyentse Wangpo.

35 Jamyang Khyentse Wangpo gave his blessings and permission to Jamgön Kongtrül Lodrö Thaye.

36 Translated by Erik Pema Kunsang

37 Translated by Erik Pema Kunsang

38 Translated by Erik Pema Kunsang

39 Translated by Erik Pema Kunsang

40 Translated by Erik Pema Kunsang

41 Translated by Erik Pema Kunsang

42 The body mandala, as taught in the *Yumkha* sadhana is as follows: The Eight Earthly Sacred Places (*gocharya*) of the Cycle of Speech—the chakra of wealth (i.e., the throat) is Lampaka, the underarms and kidney cavity are Kamarupa, the two nipples are Odra, the navel is Trishakuni, the tip of the

nose is Koshala, the palate is the country of Kalinga, the heart is Kancika, and Himalaya—and the Eight Subterranean Sacred Places (*bhugarbha*) of the Cycle of Body—the genitals are the land of Pretapuri, the anus is the land of Grihadeva, the thumbs and big toes are Maru, the thighs are Saurashtra, the calves are Suvarnadvipa, the sixteen fingers and toes are Nagara, the knees are Kulanta and Sindhu. Jigme Lingpa, *Yumkha Dechen Gyalmo, Queen of Great Bliss,* trans. Tulku Thondup, ed. Adam Peacey, (Rigpa Translations, 2012), 60.

43 Translated by Zack Beer and Marcia B. Schmidt

44 Included in this commentary are teachings not explained in Orgyen Tobgyal's commentary.

45 Erik Pema Kunsang, trans., *Guru's Heart Practices,* (San Rafael, CA: Rangjung Yeshe Publications, 2015), 27.

46 The two purities are, the purity that is inherent from the beginning and the purity of having removed all temporary obscurations. Lama Tsultrim Zangpo, oral instructions.

47 Translated by Erik Pema Kunsang

48 Translated by Erik Pema Kunsang

50 Translated by Erik Pema Kunsang

51 mkha' spyod mkha' 'gro'i lam rim gyi smon lam rdo rje'i zam pa bzhugs so

52 Orgyen Tobgyal Rinpoche, unpublished oral teachings, Rigpa Center, 1997.

53 Padmasambhava and Jamgön Kongtrül, *Light of Wisdom,* Volume 1, trans. Erik Pema Kunsang, (Hong Kong: Rangjung Yeshe Publications, 1999), 273.

54 ibid., 251–2 One list of the five tertön kings contains Nyang Ral Nyima Oser (1124–1192), Guru Chokyi Wangchuk (1212–1270), Dorje Lingpa (1346–1405), Pema Lingpa (1445/50–1521), and (Padma Ösel) Do-ngak Lingpa (Jamyang Khyentse Wangpo) (1820–1892). Sometimes the list also includes the great tertön Rigdzin Godem (1337–1408).

55 ibid., 118–122.

56 Also translated as nails.

57 Padmasambhava and Jamgön Kongtrül, *Light of Wisdom,* Volume II, trans. Erik Pema Kunsang, (Hong Kong: Rangjung Yeshe Publications, 1998), 111–115. To explain the "four stakes that bind the life force," the object to be purified is the state of affairs of a sentient being's body, speech, and mind as well as its activities. The result of purification is the body, speech, mind, qualities, and activities of buddhahood. Even though the basic state of affairs of sentient beings is primordially pure as these aspects of buddhahood, in the apparent state, they are seen as being impure and involved in the cause and effect of samsaric existence. Purification occurs by applying the key points of instruction in the four stakes that bind the life force; thereby, you will be able to realize the way it ultimately is. Thus, by binding samsara and nirvana with the life force of their purity as equals, both the basic and the apparent aspects—the practitioner's three gates and activities and the deity's

body, speech, mind, qualities, and activities—are brought onto the path as the great primordial purity. This is therefore the extraordinary key point of the unity of development and completion, and the special feature of the Old School of the Early Translations, Ngagyur Nyingma. [Dilgo Khyentse]

58 ibid., 207. An authentic image of the deity means one that has been consecrated and has the power to capture your attention. [Dilgo Khyentse]

59 ibid., 207. The five experiences that gradually occur are: the experience of movement, which is like a waterfall; the experience of attainment, which is like a river flowing in a gorge; the experience of familiarity, which is like the gentle flow of a great river; the experience of steadiness, which is like a pond undulating from a breeze; and the experience of perfection, which is like the great ocean free from waves. [Dilgo Khyentse]

60 ibid., 208. The shortcomings for samadhi are the seven faults for all types of development stage: forgetting the focus, laziness, fear of not accomplishing, dullness, agitation, the effort of being discontent even when the deity is visualized, and the lack of effort of remaining indifferent when the deity is not visualized. These are the seven general faults. [Jokyab]

To "clear them all away by applying their respective antidotes" means to be mindful, as the remedy against forgetfulness; to cultivate trust and diligence against being lazy; to focus on basic space, as the remedy against fear; to stay in bright and cool places when dull; to generate sadness and lower the gaze when agitated; to relax mentally when involved in effort; and to exert oneself when not effortful.

Likewise, when [the visualization] is either hazy, vague, or shaded, then hold up a natural crystal to cover your eyes while looking at the support for visualization. Investigate its figure and then imagine it in your mind. [Jokyab]

61 ibid., 208–9. A selection of the instructions from *Replies to Questions from Yeshe Tsogyal* are found in *Dakini Teachings* and instructions from the *Lama Gongdü* cycle are contained in *Advice from the Lotus-Born* (Hong Kong: Rangjung Yeshe Publications, 2013). Here is one quote:

Lady Tsogyal asked the Master (Padmasambhava), "How should we continuously practice the approach and accomplishment of the yidam deity?"

The Master replied, "When practicing a yidam deity, you should practice the development stage in each session. Perform the recitation in each session, make offerings, give tormas, make praises, and request the fulfillment of your wishes. Seal the practice in emptiness with the completion stage.

"At best, do eight sessions a day; as second best, do four sessions. At the least, do one session a day. Any less is not permissible. Through that, your samayas will be fulfilled, and you will receive the siddhis.

When you attain stability in development and completion, without discarding your body, it will be matured into a deity. That is called the vidyadhara level of maturation. Although your body remains as an [ordinary] human being, your mind is matured into a deity. This is like an image formed in the mold.

"When leaving your body in the bardo state, you become that particular deity, just like the image coming out of the mold. That is called the vidyadhara level of Mahamudra. The body of a practitioner is called an 'encasement,' and the moment the body is discarded, the practitioner becomes the form of the yidam deity." [EPK]

62 ibid., 209. In regard to alternating the bodily size, attributes, posture, and shape, sometimes visualize that the figure is enormous, that deer frolic on its arms and legs, fingers and toes, and that pigeons fly in and out of its nostrils, and so forth. In particular, the nine modes of the peaceful deity and the nine modes of the wrathful deity are very important. [JOKYAB]

When changing the number of deities, train in remembering that it is the magical display of the single chief figure, who manifests in the form of the retinue. When focusing only on color, visualize the shapes, and when focusing only on shapes, visualize the various colors. Or, when the deity shifts and gradually fades away, then visualize its face and arms as being very coarse. When incomplete, then deliberately visualize the incomplete parts. [JOKYAB]

63 Train in bringing forth the enhancement of mingling these three into one: deity, your mind, and dharmata. [DILGO KHYENTSE]

64 ibid., 209. Training in this way—visualizing what you perceive as having the form of the deity—ensures that you don't stray into one-sided emptiness. Utilizing the relative ensures that the two truths are unified. Abandoning fixation on a solid reality relinquishes the ordinary clinging to things as being real. By completing the subsidiary aspects of the ritual, you perfect the accumulation of merit. By visualizing the vivid features of the [deity's] bodily form, you create the direct causes for the rupakayas. By being in harmony with the way in which the fruition is, you possess the key point of spontaneously accomplishing the three kayas. These are the six key points, which are necessary to possess. [DILGO KHYENTSE]

ACKNOWLEDGEMENTS

Without my most precious teachers, I would never have known about the dynamic energy of the dakini practices. So first, I would like to thank Tulku Urgyen Rinpoche and Orgyen Tobgyal Rinpoche for having given me so many incredible teachings replete with practice guidance. Once again, the wisdom of Lama Putsi comes to light—what a great source of combined pith instructions and practical advice. Sincere appreciation goes to Neten Chokling Rinpoche for giving me the empowerment for a Kurukulle Practice, consistent advice, and sharing his beautiful Kurukulle thangka with us here.

Gratitude goes to the great lotsawa, Erik Pema Kunsang, whose most poetic translations dignify this book. Other translators have also contributed their skills: Gyurme Avertin, Lama Sean Price, Lama Chönam, Sangye Khandro, and Han Kop. Special thanks to Dickey Wangmo for helping me with difficult points in both Tulku Urgyen Rinpoche and Orgyen Tobgyal's oral instructions. Then there is the rest of the team, whose work has enhanced *Dakini Activity* and has made such a publication possible: Anne Paniagua, for sharp and precise editing; Joan Olson, who handles the multiple variant texts; the most conscientious proofreaders, Lynn Schroeder and Michael Yockey; the unbelievably talented Lowell Boyers, for allowing his incredible painting to grace the cover designed by Mary Sweet; and the invaluable photos from Graham Sunstein. Heartfelt gratefulness is offered to Eric Colombel and *The Tsadra Foundation* for support for the preparation and printing of this book.

The joy of working with such precious material and talented people is like a celebration. May the dakinis be pleased and may they bestow blessings, accomplishments, and the power to fulfill the activities for the benefit of beings and the Dharma.

For information regarding video and audio recordings, published teachings and programs in the lineage of the Chokling Tersar, please access the following websites:

www.lotustreasure.com

www.rangjung.com

Rangjung Yeshe Publications and Translations

www.shedrub.org
Shedrub Development Mandala

www.tsoknyirinpoche.org
Tsoknyi Rinpoche Activities and Teachings

www.CGLF.org
Chokgyur Lingpa Foundation

www.erikpemakunsang.com
Works of Erik Pema Kunsang

www.all-otr.org
Teachings of Orgyen Tobgyal Rinpoche